Volume B

Focus on Grammar

WORKBOOK

An **ADVANCED** Course for Reference and Practice

Rachel Spack Koch

Longman

**Focus on Grammar: An Advanced Course
for Reference and Practice Workbook, Volume B**

Copyright © 1995 by Addison-Wesley Publishing Company, Inc.
All rights reserved.
No part of this publication may be reproduced,
stored in a retrieval system, or transmitted in any
form or by any means, electronic, mechanical,
photocopying, recording, or otherwise, without
the prior permission of the publisher.

Editorial Director: Joanne Dresner
Development Editor: Randee Falk
Production Editor: Andrea West
Production Management: Circa 86
Text Design: Six West Design
Cover Design: A Good Thing

ISBN 201-82587-2

1 2 3 4 5 6 7 8 9 10-CRS-9998979695

Contents

Part V: Adverbials and Discourse Connectors   82

Unit 12   Adverb Clauses   82

Unit 13   Adverbials: Viewpoint, Focus, and Negative   88

Unit 14   Other Discourse Connectors   94

Unit 15   Adverbial Modifying Phrases   100

Part VI: Adjective Clauses   105

Unit 16   Review and Expansion   105

Unit 17   Adjective Clauses with Quantifiers; Adjectival Modifying Phrases   113

Part VII: Noun Clauses   120

Unit 18   Noun Clauses: Subjects and Objects   120

Unit 19   Complementation   125

Part VIII: Unreal Conditions   130

Unit 20   Unreal Conditionals and Other Ways to Express Unreality   130

Unit 21   Inverted and Implied Conditionals; Subjunctive in Noun Clauses   138

Answer Key   AK 1

Tests   T 1

Units 12–15   T 1

Units 16–17   T 6

Units 18–19   T 11

Units 20–21   T 16

Answer Key for Tests   AKT 1

About the Author

Rachel Spack Koch has taught ESL, developed ESL materials, and served as grammar coordinator at the University of Miami for more than twenty years. She has also taught ESL at Harvard University, at Bellevue Community College, and at Miami-Dade Community College. In addition to *Focus on Grammar: An Advanced Course for Reference and Practice Workbook,* she has contributed to other widely used ESL workbooks and has written structure and writing questions for the TOEFL. Currently, she serves as comonitor of the ENGL-SL student list, a global educational interchange for students and teachers on the Internet.

Volume B

Focus on Grammar

WORKBOOK

An **ADVANCED** Course for Reference and Practice

UNIT 12: Adverb Clauses

PART V: ADVERBIALS AND DISCOURSE CONNECTORS

1. Identifying Adverb Clauses

World Review interviewed Dr. Milton Scope, a professor of sociology and an expert in what makes happy families. Underline all the adverb clauses in the interview and indicate what kind each is by giving it one of the following labels: reason, contrast, condition, time, place, comparison, result.

WORLD REVIEW

WR: Dr. Scope, just what *does* make a happy family?

SCOPE: There is a cliche that all happy families have some things in common. <u>While this may be trite</u> *(contrast)*, it is also true.

WR: Really? What are these things?

SCOPE: Well, in happy families, although family members may argue, they have a basic concern for each other. This factor is very important because every person needs to know that somebody cares for and about him or her.

WR: Is this caring enough to keep young people from turning to criminal acts and violence?

SCOPE: No. Of course it's not that simple, but if a person feels connected to another, he or she is more likely to act in socially acceptable ways.

WR: So, is being connected the principal factor?

SCOPE: It is important.

WR: Tell us what else is important.

SCOPE: When family members have goals and support each other's goals, the family feels united.

WR: Give us an example.

SCOPE: Well, if a parent is hoping to be promoted at work, everybody is supportive and shows interest. If a youngster is trying to make the basketball team, the other family members show encouragement and warmth.

WR: What happens in times of trouble?

SCOPE: When one family member is having trouble, the others should exhibit concern and try to help. Suppose, for example, that someone is fired from a job. Even though this person doesn't have a job, he or she should still feel valued by the rest of the family. In fact, precisely because this person doesn't have a job, he or she *needs* to feel valued.

WR: So, is that the key word, *valued*?

SCOPE: I think it is. People need to feel valued, appreciated. They also need to feel secure among the family members. They need to feel so secure that they know their families will always be there for them.

WR: Does the economic status of the family matter?

SCOPE: Of course, economic stability is favorable. But happy families exist wherever you look, in all economic strata. And unhappy families as well.

2. Using Adverb Clauses

Read the following captions for items included in a mail-order catalog sent out around Christmas time. Complete each caption by filling in the blanks with the item in the box that will form an appropriate adverb clause.

when you want	wherever he goes	so fascinating that
if she likes	less than	as soon as
because it is necessary for her		less expensive than

1. _Because it is necessary for her_ to have a computer for all her work, even when she travels, you must get her this exceptional new laptop.

2. For the whole family, this deluxe picnic cooler will prove perfect _____ the warmer weather arrives.

(continued on next page)

3. _____ on his business trips, he will want to take this compact suitcase on wheels.

4. For the home, this wide-screen television with stereo is _____ ever before.

5. _____ to tell her that you love her very much and want to marry her, present her with a beautiful diamond like this.

6. Our new lightweight aluminum fishing rod weighs _____ any other fishing rod and will make him a very happy fisherman.

7. _____ to prepare many kinds of interesting dishes, delight her with this versatile food processor.

8. For the children, our 1,000-piece set of interlocking plastic pieces will be _____ your little ones will be kept occupied for hours.

3. Using Adverb Clauses

The following is a recorded message for an airline ticket office. Complete the message by filling in the blanks with the words from the box that correctly introduce the adverb clauses. Use each item only once.

as soon as	if	until
because	so	wherever
even though	than	while

Thank you for calling Global Airlines. ___*Because*___ the demand for our new,
                                              1.
affordable fares is so heavy, our agents are not available to assist you now. Please be patient.
_____ an agent is available, you will be connected. _____
        2.   3.
you are connected, we will keep you entertained with music and will provide some information of interest to you.

_____ you want to go, you can get there on Global Airlines. You don't
        4.
have to put up with winter, _____ it's winter all around you. In fact,
                                     5.

_____ the weather is cold and you don't like it, then a Caribbean vacation may
       6.
be just the thing for you. Global has more flights to the Caribbean _____ any
                                                                          7.
other airline. Make your reservations now _____ the supply of low-fare tickets
                                                  8.
lasts. Our fares are _____ reasonable you can take your whole family along
                           9.
with you.

4. Forming Complex Sentences with Adverb Clauses

Combine each pair of sentences to form a single complex sentence. Use the indicated subordinating conjunction, so that the combined sentence will be logical. Do not change any words in the sentences.

1. There is a lot of violence today.

   No one can escape being touched by it. (because)

   Because there is a lot of violence today, no one can escape being touched by it.

2. We turn on the television.

   We are bombarded with scenes and stories of violence. (whenever)

   _____

3. We go out.

   We know it is possible that we will become victims of violence. (when)

   _____

4. An ever-increasing amount of money is being spent to combat crime.

   Crime rates have not fallen. (in spite of the fact that)

   _____

5. The public can't agree on how to fight crime.

   There is little that can really be done. (as long as)

   _____

6. We need to understand violence better.

   We are searching for its causes. (because)

   _____

7. Children in strong families tend to become socially responsible citizens.

   We need to take steps to strengthen the family. (since)

   _____

5. Editing

Read the following draft about the history of sports that was prepared for a parks-department bulletin. Find and correct the ten errors in the use of adverb clauses.

             they
When wanted to take a break from the serious business of self-preservation, early humans engaged in some type of sports. The playing of games is an important factor distinguishing the higher orders of living things on the evolutionary scale from the lower ones. While animals on the lower end of the scale they display the least amount of playfulness, those at the higher end display the most. If when we watch amoebas through a microscope or earthworms on the ground, they do not appear to play at all; however, dogs, cats, and certainly dolphins and human children play extensively.

Sports are different from other pastimes because wherever conformity to agreed-upon, prescribed rules is required. Whether the sport it is individual or group, these rules must be followed. And when the rules are defined and agreed on, you have a game.

Stone arrowheads discovered by archaeologists indicate that archery was a hunting skill in primordial days, long before became a popular competitive sport in the third century. Games that were precursors of basketball, soccer, and bowling took place wherever was there enough space for a field. Henry VIII coerced court members into playing tennis. Whenever and wherever they are played, sports engage many in healthy competition.

Today, sports are of so interest that many millions of people play and watch them. Although young people are especially interested in sports, sports are an excellent way to keep them out of trouble. Involvement in sports channels young people's energies towards socially acceptable activities and away from crime. Because that you want to have a place for your children to play, you should support your Parks Department. *

---

* Based on Richard B. Manchester, *Amazing Facts,* (New York: Bristol Park Books, 1991).

6. Personalization

What do you think are some of the main factors that contribute to crime? Write a short essay giving your views. Include some of the phrases in the box.

> A person may turn to crime if . . .
>
> Whenever people are unemployed, . . .
>
> Because guns are readily available, . . .
>
> There is so much violence on television that . . .
>
> Crime among young people may be increasing because . . .
>
> Where laws are strictly enforced, . . .
>
> Crime will continue to increase unless . . .
>
> We will have much less crime when . . .

UNIT 13

Adverbials: Viewpoint, Focus, and Negative

1. Identifying Viewpoint, Focus, and Negative Adverbials

Read the following letter. Underline the twenty-nine viewpoint, focus, and negative adverbials.

Dear Ricardo,

I'm <u>really</u> glad that you took the job as night clerk in the hotel. I think things will work out for you. Just be serious, work hard, and study hard. By the time your semester ends, you will have saved up almost enough money to get yourself out of debt.

Unfortunately, life is not going so well for me here in my relationship with Lisa. In fact, I hardly have a relationship with her. I think about only her almost every minute, and now I scarcely see her. Not only does she refuse to go out with me, but she doesn't return my phone calls. Never in my whole life have I met anybody like Lisa, and never have I been so miserable. Obviously, she is not interested in me, and I don't know what I did to turn her off. Maybe she simply got bored with me. Maybe she thinks I'm merely a student in transit and not worth an investment of her time. Luckily, as I told you, I have made some friends here, but rarely do they call me these days, because I seem so depressed all the time. Actually, Ricardo, I really am depressed. I know that there are other girls besides Lisa. A few girls who know me even invited me to their homes for dinner, but clearly, I can't go out with them. I guess I'm just a prisoner of love—an unrequited love.

Frankly, I don't care about anything at all these days. Little does Lisa know how miserable I am, and if she finds out, I guess she won't call me. But, if she does call, even just to say hello, I'll be the happiest man in the world. Only when that happens will I be able to live like a normal person again.

Marco

ADVERBIALS: VIEWPOINT, FOCUS, AND NEGATIVE ▼ 89

2. Using Focus Adverbs

Rewrite the sentences in this ad for a political candidate by inserting each focus adverb in an appropriate place—that is, right before the words or phrase it focuses on. (Where items include a second sentence, this sentence is intended to clarify the focus.)

Aren't you fed up with the incompetent and corrupt politicians in office? The time has come to throw the rascals out! Ron Rong and all his cronies have almost ruined our state. But Don Deare has come along just in time to save us!
Do you know some of the things Ron Rong has done?

1. He said he wanted to do what was best for the state. (only) He didn't want to do anything else.
   He said he wanted to do only what was best for the state.

2. But he used up the state's money. (really)
   _____

3. He put his cronies in the best jobs. (only) Nobody else got these jobs.
   _____

4. He did everything he could for his cronies; he paid for their so-called business trips. (even)
   _____

5. He did the minimal work. (merely) He never did any more work than that minimum.
   _____

6. He appeared in his office, dispensed favors, and went out to play golf. (simply)
   _____

7. He didn't care about the people of this state. (just)
   _____

8. This state will be saved if you elect Don Deare. (only)
   _____

3. Using Negative Adverbs

The following sentences are from another ad for the same political candidate. Rewrite the sentences, inserting the negative adverbs at the beginning and making any other changes in form that are needed.

1. Don Deare loves the people; he acts to help them. (Not only/but)

   Not only does Don Deare love the people, but he acts to help them.

He works almost 365 days a year.

2. He takes a vacation. (Seldom)

   _____

His wonderful and loving family would like to have him spend more time at home.

3. He is able to spend much time with them. (Rarely)

   _____

Although he is not able to spend enough time with his family, he is a loving and considerate husband and father.

4. He neglects his family. (Never)

   _____

He is an honest man.

5. He would accept a bribe. (On no account)

   _____

He makes informed decisions. He looks at each problem carefully.

6. He makes a decision. (Only then)

   _____

7. People realize how many hours he has volunteered at the shelter for the homeless. (Little)

   _____

8. He thinks of himself first. (Never)

   _____

9. He has served the people very well as a civic volunteer; he will do even more for them as a senator. (Not only/but)

   _____

Vote for Don Deare!

4. Using Viewpoint, Focus, and Negative Adverbials

Read the following speech made to a group of parents. Rewrite the sentences so that they include the adverbs indicated. Where two or three blank lines are given, rewrite the sentence in two or three ways.

Welcome, parents.

1. We are pleased that attention is being focused on the importance of strong families. (certainly)
   A. *Certainly, we are pleased that attention is being focused on the importance of strong families.*
   B. *We are certainly pleased that attention is being focused on the importance of strong families.*
   C. *We are pleased, certainly, that attention is being focused on the importance of strong families.*

2. We agree that steps must be taken to strengthen the family. (clearly)
   _____

3. There is another factor that must be considered, however— the influence of TV violence. (sadly)
   A. _____
   B. _____

4. We encounter scenes of violence wherever we look, in cartoon shows and programs for families. (even)
   _____

5. Our children can't help seeing these scenes. (unfortunately)
   A. _____
   B. _____
   C. _____

6. We must take action to strengthen the family, we must pressure our legislators to stop TV violence. (not only/but)
   _____

7. Much needs to be done. (obviously)
   A. _____
   B. _____
   C. _____

8. We will win the war against violent programs. (hopefully)
   A. _____
   B. _____
   C. _____

9. We can limit our children's TV viewing. (fortunately)
   A. _____
   B. _____
   C. _____

(continued on next page)

10. This means allowing programs that do not show violence. (only)

_____

11. Other programs are "off limits." (simply)

_____

12. We also have to help our children develop other interests so they will not be tempted to sit glued to the TV. (at all)

_____

5. Editing

Read the following draft of an article. Find and correct the nineteen errors in the use of viewpoint, focus, and negative adverbials.

      This week in Los Angeles, California, the top Scrabble players of the world are locked together in mortal conflict. Scrabble players? Scrabble players, indeed. Here ~~are they~~ *they are*, and they are battling hard really to determine the world's champion. This is a tournament for the only best players of this word game; seldom amateurs appear here. The game of Scrabble is played throughout the world and in six different languages. The object is simply to score as many points as possible by forming words from the individual letters imprinted on little wooden squares. A player hopefully gets many points by making clever combinations of letters according to the rules of the game. The competition at the tournament is as just fierce as that at the World Cup or the Olympic Games. A player never gives nothing to the opposing player; each point is won through only a hard fight.

      In playing Scrabble, not only it is necessary to have an extensive vocabulary, but it is also imperative to possess a good imagination and excellent mathematical skills. Mathematical skills? Yes. To obviously know the words is important, but it is more even important to know how just to place the letters on the board and to estimate the probabilities of drawing the letters you want at any given time.

      Of the top ten Scrabble players, one only is engaged in a career that requires language skills. Almost all the others are mathematics and computer professionals, and even there is a croupier among them. At all this is not the image we have of people obsessed with words; people obsessed with words are supposed to be writers, poets, and English teachers, not practical and precise mathematical types.

      This doesn't mean that mathematical wizards play only this game. At the National Scrabble Tournament, held semiannually in different cities of the United States, one also finds doctors, lawyers, schoolteachers, surfers, truck drivers, business people, retirees, and teenagers, among many others.

One hundred sixty-seven actually different occupations were listed for the 400 people who participated in the last tournament.

Little it is known that this subculture of Scrabble players exists. It surely does exist, though, with its hundreds of participants training and practicing, memorizing lists, and learning strategies as just vigorously as marathon runners preparing for their race.

6. Personalization

How do you think you and one other person could survive for a year in the wilderness? What would you take with you? What would you do? Write a paragraph about this topic. Include some of the phrases in the box.

> We will take only . . .
>
> We won't even take . . .
>
> Fortunately, we are . . .
>
> During this time, we will just . . .
>
> Rarely . . .
>
> Certainly, with strength and a little luck . . .
>
> Hopefully, . . .

UNIT 14

Other Discourse Connectors

1. Identifying Discourse Connectors

Read the following installment of "Around the Stars," a one-minute television spot about news and gossip from Hollywood. Underline the twenty-one discourse connectors.

Good evening, ladies and gentlemen. We are here to bring you the latest news from Hollywood.

<u>First</u>, a major new studio has been created. The three biggest motion picture producers have just joined forces to form a new studio. As a result, Bigthree Productions, as it is going to be named, will be the largest studio ever in Hollywood. Moreover, it has more money behind it than any studio in Hollywood has ever had. In addition, seven megastars have joined the group as limited partners; therefore, they will have a financial interest in the success of the company. Bigthree Productions is expected to produce excellent financial results even at the beginning. However, there are several lawsuits pending against the three partners from the complicated business dealings they had with their previous studios. In fact, one of the lawsuits has been brought by the first ex-wife of one of the partners, who claims that her husband owes her $7 million for her starring role in *Imelda*.

Next, we have reports that movie queen Rosalinda Rock has finally found happiness. Yes, she and actor Fox Craft were married secretly last month in a small town in Nevada. There had been reports that Fox was involved with an Italian starlet, but these reports have turned out to be false. Rosalinda and Fox are getting a beachfront house in Santa Monica and a ranch near Sun Valley, so they will have a choice about where to spend their time between movies. Fox gave Rosalinda a diamond-and-emerald necklace as a wedding present; besides that, he had apparently given her a ten-carat diamond ring several weeks earlier. Rosalinda says she wants to have many children and stay home, at one of her homes, to take care of them; nevertheless, she is off to Tahiti next week for several months on location.

Finally, nobody can predict this year who the winners of the Academy Awards are going to be. For one thing, the pictures this year were better than ever before. The adventure story *Running in Space* has stunned everyone with its special effects, and it has impressed the critics with its incredible plot. It's a definite contender for the best picture award, along with *Love at the Turn of the Century,* which moved even the most macho of men to tears. On the other hand, the award could go to any one of several fine comedies, or the brilliant horror movie *Drackenstein* might be the first of its genre to win.

The suspense over the Academy Awards is tremendous, and everybody is eagerly awaiting the big night. Meanwhile, join us again every night at 9:00 to learn more of what's really going on Around the Stars.

2. Using Discourse Connectors

Read the following letter, written by a freshman in college. Complete the letter by filling in the blanks with discourse connectors from the box. (Each connector should be used once.) Do not change punctuation.

however	but	as a result	in contrast
third	first	to sum up	and
for example	also	second	

Dear Mom and Dad,

It's great to be here on campus. _____However_____ (1), there is something I really need, and that is a car.

The town does have a bus, _____ (2) this bus comes very infrequently. _____ (3), I've found myself in three undesirable situations. _____ (4), I've been stuck in the dorm. _____ (5), I've gotten rides with other people and have had to go when and where they wanted to go. _____ (6), I've walked into town and taken hours to do what I could have done in minutes. On Saturday, _____ (7), I spent all day buying some groceries. _____ (8), not having a car has been extremely inconvenient.

With a car, _____ (9), life would be easy, _____ (10) I would probably have much more time to do my schoolwork. _____ (11), with a car I could come visit you more often.

Please give this matter some thought, Mom and Dad. I'll call you on Sunday.

Your loving daughter,

Nicole

3. Using Discourse Connectors

Complete the following article by filling in each blank with the correct discourse connector.

HURRICANES AND EARTHQUAKES

Hurricanes and earthquakes are similar in that they both cause extensive damage. _____*However*_____, an earthquake is even more terrifying than a hurricane just because it
1. (However / Because of / In addition)

strikes so suddenly. An earthquake gives no warning, _____ there is plenty of warning
2. (and / but / or)

before a hurricane. Weather satellites, _____, send signals enabling the
3. (in fact / in conclusion / on the other hand)

weather bureau to issue warnings several days in advance of a hurricane. _____,
4. (As a result / On the contrary / Yet)

people can prepare for hurricanes by stocking up on food and supplies and securing their property.

_____, there is enough time for people who live near the coastal areas to
5. (Furthermore / However / Consequently)

evacuate to higher land if they are advised to do so by the authorities. _____,
6. (Consequently / Therefore / In contrast)

because earthquakes give no warning, preparation is impossible. _____, many
7. (Moreover / Therefore / After that)

buildings in earthquake zones are not built strongly enough to withstand the shock waves of a strong

quake, _____ they are vulnerable to damage. People are not safe in their homes,
8. (instead / so / but)

_____ can they seek safety on the highways, which can also be damaged by the shock waves.
9. (or / nor / and)

4. Using Discourse Connectors

Complete the following by filling in each blank with the correct discourse connector. Take the punctuation into consideration.

Dear Marco,
    Now I'm really worried about you. I'm the one who's always asking for advice,

_____*and*_____ you're the one who's always giving it. _____,
1. (and / additionally)   2. (Also / Instead)

this time I find myself advising you.

_____, no matter what, you have to get a hold of yourself.
3. (First / Next)

_____, you are going to spiral downward and feel worse and worse.
4. (Therefore / Otherwise)

_____, you won't be effective in this downbeat mood that you're in.
5. (However / In addition)

_____ _____, Lisa or any other young woman you
6. (And / But)   7. (first / finally)

may meet is going to find you a drag, _____ you'll definitely find
8. (however / so)

yourself without a girlfriend.

_____ feeling so bad, you've got to get out in the world again.
9. (Despite / On the contrary)

_____, you should take one of the young women up on her offer to
10. (However / For instance)

invite you to dinner. Who knows? _____ having a good dinner, you
11. (Along with / Likewise)

might find a really pleasant relationship.

Now, enough about you. Let's get back to me. I got fired. I was doing everything

right, _____ I still got fired. It was a terrible experience.
12. (finally / but)

_____, it couldn't have happened at a worse time: I'd just found out my
13. (Thus / Besides)

landlord is raising the rent.

Hope to hear some better news from you.

Ricardo

5. Editing

Read the following draft of a composition for a freshman English class. Find and correct the eleven errors in the use of discourse connectors. Replace the incorrect discourse connectors; do not change word order or punctuation.

I like to play football for a lot of reasons.

First, I like the teamwork. It really feels good to be part of a group whose members depend on each other. For example, when I throw the ball to a receiver on my team, I know that there's a good chance he's going to catch it. It takes both of us to make the catch work. ~~Accordingly~~ *Because of* my good throwing ability, the ball is usually on target; however, the receiver also has to be in position and has to make

(continued on next page)

the catch. Because, our score is due in part to me as the quarterback, in part to the receiver, and in part to the other members of the team.

Second, I like the competition. I like the feeling of playing to win; and, I like the sense of fighting the other team.

Third, I like the physical exercise. I think pushing myself to my physical limit is good for my body. I am not afraid of overdoing the exercise, or do I have fears of being hurt during a game, however the fact that many quarterbacks get hurt.

Finally, I like the glory. I love it when the crowd roars to encourage us, also I love it when I hear the cheerleaders shouting my name. It sure makes a guy feel important to be recognized around town as a big hero.

Are there any drawbacks? Yes. It's terrific to play football, nevertheless there are some negative aspects. Being part of a team is great; but, you don't have much of a private life. Playing in competition is exciting. Although, you don't get much chance to relax. In fact, there's a negative aspect to each of the things I like about football, but these drawbacks are relatively unimportant.

In conclusion, I like being a football player consequently the teamwork, the competition, the physical exercise, and the glory.

6. Personalization

Participation in sports is often required in schools and colleges. Some people think that these activities should not be compulsory. Write a three-paragraph essay about the pros and cons of requiring participation in sports. Include the sentences given below, and use some of the discourse connectors in the box.

Discourse connectors:

	Moreover	Despite	Otherwise	Second
In addition	For example/instance	In contrast	As a result	Finally
Furthermore	However	Therefore	First	

Paragraph 1: There are certain reasons why schools should require participation in sports activities.

Paragraph 2: On the other hand, there are also reasons why participation in sports activities should not be required.

Paragraph 3: I think the advantages of requiring participation outweigh the disadvantages. OR
I think the disadvantages of requiring participation outweigh the advantages.

Paragraph 3 last sentence: In conclusion, . . .

UNIT 15

Adverbial Modifying Phrases

1. Identifying Adverbial Modifying Phrases

Read the following editorial article from a local newspaper and underline the adverbial modifying phrases.

Our beautiful city, Beautiville, has become too popular. <u>Known for its clean air, friendly people, excellent transportation, and safe streets</u>, Beautiville naturally tends to attract newcomers. We in Beautiville are proud of our city's reputation but—and this is a big but—are concerned that its population has doubled in only five years. While struggling with the demands presented by a population grown too fast, the government has attempted to serve everybody well. However, these attempts have been inadequate, creating more problems than solutions. Having caused such strains that our government can no longer effectively serve us, this increase in population now should be limited.

How can we do this? We can do it by limiting the number of high-density buildings permitted to be built in certain areas. We can do it by discouraging outsiders from investing in our city. By taking concrete measures like these, we can effectively limit our growth. Faced with a tough choice between limiting our population and letting our standards of living slip, we must take positive steps and preserve the excellent quality of life that we have here in Beautiville.

2. Using Adverbial Modifying Phrases

Read the following passage (a continuation of the "Hurricanes and Earthquakes" article in Unit 14). Complete the article by filling in each blank with the correct words.

Both hurricanes and earthquakes can severely disrupt normal life _____*by damaging*_____ the infrastructure in the area.
    1. (by damaging / having damaging / damage)

_____ cut off, the electricity, the telephones, and the
    2. (Been / Having been / To be)

water service remain nonfunctioning, sometimes for several weeks after the event has occurred.

_____ its electricity, the community has no refrigeration, and so keeping
3. (By lost / Having been lost / Having lost)

food safe from contamination becomes a serious problem. _____ a
4. (To ensure / By ensuring / Having ensured)

continuous supply of vital electricity, hospitals are equipped with generators that can provide

it in the event of a power outage. Without electricity, the traffic signals might not function, and

_____ these signals, drivers frequently have accidents and create traffic
5. (not having / not having had / not to have)

jams. When _____ so continuously, people often act rudely to each other,
6. (stressed / stressing / having stressed)

further _____ the discomfort.
7. (spreading / spread / having spread)

To summarize, the widespread loss of electricity and other services following a disaster such

as a hurricane or an earthquake affects people very seriously, often _____
8. (having brought / bringing / to bring)

chaos to the community.

3. Forming Sentences with Adverbial Phrases

Combine each pair of sentences to make a single sentence, in which the first sentence becomes an adverbial phrase and the second sentence an independent clause. Use present participles, past participles, and **having** *plus past participles as appropriate. You may move the noun subject to the second clause to replace the subject. Do not add any words.*

1. Many people try to stay healthy. They quickly adopt the latest health recommendations.

   Trying to stay healthy, many people quickly adopt the latest health recommendations.

2. People were told that vitamin C, vitamin E, and beta-carotene greatly reduce cancer risk. They began buying these nutrients in large quantities.

   _____

   _____

3. People were informed that taking one aspirin a day lessens the chances of having a heart attack. They began taking aspirin.

   _____

   _____

(continued on next page)

4. Many people learned that one glass of wine per day has a beneficial effect on the heart and circulatory system. They now drink wine for medicinal reasons.

5. People hope to lower their cholesterol levels. They minimize their intake of animal fats.

6. People know that roughage in the diet is excellent for digestion. They are consuming more fresh fruit, vegetables, and whole wheat products.

7. Some people believe that eating a lot of fish will raise their intelligence level. They eat a lot of fish.

8. People have known for a long time that too much salt and sugar is unhealthful. They buy a lot of salt-free and sugar-free products.

9. People realize that they can contribute to their own good health. They eat much more knowledgeably than they used to.

4. Editing

*The following message greets new users of a computer communications program.
Find and correct the eleven errors in the adverbial phrases.*

Welcome to the wonderful world of Globe Probe! With our computer communications program you will quickly be able to find exactly what you want just by click*ing* on the easily identifiable icon for your area of interest. Found more information, games, and new friends than you ever dreamed of, you will enter a brand new life. Hit *Enter* to continued with this message.

After having complete the tour of what's available on Globe Probe, explore each of our departments. What are your interests? Sports? When look around to find the latest on sports, you will find discussion groups, news groups, and hot-off-the-press scores in our sports department. Finance? Get the business news as well as the latest in stock quotes.

Scroll through a listing of 103 of America's most popular publications. Having find the publication you want, peruse the article titles and just click on your choice. Shopping? Movie reviews? Concerts? Book reviews? Travel? Just to clicking on *Imprints*, you will immediately be able to read reviews of the newest happenings by the most knowledgeable writers in their fields.

Then, participate in one or more of our clubs: the environment, astronomy, foreign affairs, science fiction, and twenty-eight more. You will find hundreds of other people with the same interests. Having join a club, you will encounter a whole new world of friends and communication.

Our encyclopedia is the most comprehensive of all the online services. When require to find facts fast, simply access the topic you want to know about—the latest research on tooth decay, for example, or what the capital of Belize is—and you'll find the facts you need.

Have obtained the facts so quickly and easily, you will be amazed by how much you can learn while have a lot of fun at the same time. Globe Probe immeasurably enriches your life from the first moment that you use it.

Hit the space bar to view the Globe Probe menu.

5. Personalization

What are your career goals for the next ten years? Write a short essay about what your goals are and how you will achieve them. Include some of the adverbial clauses in the box. Be sure to avoid dangling modifiers.

> When thinking about my career goals for the next ten years, . . .
>
> Having thought about my career goals for the next ten years, . . .
>
> If given the opportunity . . .
>
> By working hard, . . .
>
> When given a job to do, . . .
>
> If forced to do boring or unpleasant tasks, . . .
>
> While performing my duties, . . .
>
> To gain recognition, . . .
>
> Having achieved my goals, . . .
>
> Hoping to improve even further, . . .

PART VI: ADJECTIVE CLAUSES

1. Identifying Adjective Clauses

Read the following article about an invention and its inventor. Underline all the adjective clauses. (Remember, some adjective clauses do not have a relative pronoun.)

What do you know about Liquid Paper? Liquid Paper is the white liquid <u>that covers up the mistakes</u> you make when writing or typing. It was invented by Bette Nesmith Graham, a secretary in Dallas in the early 1950s, who began using tempera paint to cover up her typing errors.

At the time, she was a 27-year-old single mother of one son, struggling to make ends meet and working as a secretary to the chairman of a big Dallas bank. When she found herself confronted with her first electric typewriter, whose ink didn't erase as cleanly as that of manual typewriters, Ms. Nesmith, who was also an artist, quietly began painting out her mistakes. Soon she was supplying bottles of her homemade preparation, which she called Mistake Out, to other secretaries in the building.

When she lost her job with the company, she turned to working full-time to develop the Mistake Out as a business, expanding from her house into a small trailer she had bought for the backyard. In hopes of marketing her product, she approached IBM, which turned her down. She stepped up her own marketing and within a decade was a financial success. The product, which came to be called Liquid Paper, was manufactured in four countries and sold in nearly three dozen. In fiscal 1979, which ended about six months before she sold the company, it had sales of $38 million, of which $3.5 million was net income. By the time she finally sold her business to Gillette in 1979, she had built her simple, practical idea into a $47.5 million business.

It is heartwarming that the story has a happy ending in more ways than one. Ms. Nesmith remarried and became Mrs. Graham. Her son, Michael, a musician of whom she is understandably proud, became very successful as one of a music group called "The Monkees," which appeared on an NBC television show for several years in the mid-1960s.

(continued on next page)

UNIT 16

Review and Expansion

Subsequently a country-rock musician, a songwriter, and a video producer, he now heads a production company in California, where he also directs some charities.

With some of her profits, Mrs. Graham established a foundation whose purpose is to provide leading intellectuals with the time, space, and compatible colleagues that they need to ponder and articulate the most important social problems of our era. Bette Nesmith Graham first developed a product that there was clearly a need for; then she used the substantial profits for charitable purposes, which is a fine thing to do.*

*Based on an article by Eric Morgenthaler from, *The Wall Street Journal,* July 29, 1994.

2. Using Relative Pronouns

Complete the article by filling in the blanks with appropriate relative pronouns from the box. Where more than one selection is possible, write all the possibilities, including **0** if no relative pronoun is needed.

who	which	that
whom	whose	when
where	0	

Dr. Jennifer Wise has obtained a grant of $17 million for her research on the factors affecting the natural resistance __that / which / 0__ (1.) the human body has to cold viruses. Dr. Wise has investigated the common beliefs about catching colds to _____ (2.) people have long subscribed—for example, the beliefs that colds come from sitting in places _____ (3.) there is a draft, going out with wet hair, not wearing warm enough clothing, and sitting near a person _____ (4.) is coughing and sneezing.

She discredits all these ideas as having no merit but says that there are other factors _____ (5.) actually contribute to catching a cold. For example, her research has shown that you can catch a cold from a person _____ (6.) you have been near just from touching him or her or something _____ (7.) he or she has touched, so it is important and effective to wash your hands frequently and well.

Second, not getting the rest _____ (8.) your body needs lowers resistance. People _____ (9.) sleep patterns don't provide them with enough deep sleep will more easily catch a cold than people _____ (10.) get enough rest. Deep sleep is especially important at times _____ (11.) people are under more stress than usual.

Third, she has found some evidence that taking high doses of vitamin C, _____ (12.) has been controversial for some time, actually does seem to raise resistance.

As for treating the common cold: Nothing will cure it, but there are some palliative steps _____ (13.) may be taken. You may take aspirin and other medications _____ (14.) act to relieve your discomfort, stay in bed if you can, drink plenty of liquids, and partake of the home remedy _____ (15.) has been around for centuries: the chicken soup _____ (16.) your mother makes.

3. Using Adjective Clauses

Write sentences describing ten objects that are part of modern life. First match each item in column I with the appropriate item in column II. Then, for each pair of matched items, write a sentence that uses an adjective clause to describe the object. (Some adjective clauses may be written in more than one way.)

I

1. A cellular phone/wireless telephone
2. A beeper/battery-operated device
3. An air bag/device in a car
4. A microwave oven/oven
5. A fax machine/machine
6. A computer/electronic device
7. A CD/small disc
8. An answering machine/electronic device
9. An electronic dictionary/gadget
10. A VCR/machine

II

A. transmits written material instantly by telephone
B. it records telephone messages
C. it records TV shows for viewing at a future time
D. you find words in it by punching in their letters
E. it inflates upon collision to prevent injury
F. people use it to speak to others from their cars
G. its function is to store and process data
H. its beeping noise indicates when someone is trying to make a phone connection with you
I. music is recorded on it
J. people cook food quickly in it

1. F. A cellular telephone is a wireless telephone that people use to speak to others from their cars.

2. _____

3. _____

4. _____

5. _____

6. _____

7. _____
   _____

8. _____
   _____

9. _____
   _____

10. _____
    _____

4. Distinguishing between Identifying and Nonidentifying Clauses

Read the following sentences about the Moonrise Film Festival. Each of the sentences contains an adjective clause of either the identifying or nonidentifying type. For each, decide whether (A) or (B) describes the first sentence. Pay special attention to punctuation.

1. Moviegoers, who appreciate fine films, were very satisfied with the Moonrise Film Festival this year.

   (A.) Moviegoers in general appreciate fine films.

   B. Only some moviegoers appreciate fine films.

2. Moviegoers who appreciate fine films were very satisfied with the Moonrise Film Festival this year.

   A. Moviegoers in general appreciate fine films.

   B. Only some moviegoers appreciate fine films.

3. The films, which were chosen for their artistry in cinematography, left vivid and lasting impressions.

   A. The films in general left vivid and lasting impressions.

   B. Only some films left vivid and lasting impressions.

4. The films that were chosen for their artistry in cinematography left vivid and lasting impressions.

   A. The films in general left vivid and lasting impressions.

   B. Only some films left vivid and lasting impressions.

5. Offbeat films brought critical acclaim to directors, who are normally very profit oriented.

   A. Directors in general are normally very profit oriented.

   B. Only some directors are normally very profit oriented.

(continued on next page)

6. Offbeat films brought critical acclaim to directors who are normally very profit oriented.

   A. Directors in general are normally very profit oriented.

   B. Only some directors are normally very profit oriented.

7. In the animation category, the audience was surprised and satisfied by Hollywood's new-style cartoons, which address serious social concerns.

   A. Hollywood's new-style cartoons in general address social concerns.

   B. Only some of Hollywood's new-style cartoons address social concerns.

8. In the animation category, the audience was surprised and satisfied by Hollywood's new-style cartoons that address serious social concerns.

   A. Hollywood's new-style cartoons in general address social concerns.

   B. Only some of Hollywood's new-style cartoons address social concerns.

9. The foreign entries, which were brilliantly directed, unfortunately may not succeed at the box office here.

   A. The foreign entries in general were brilliantly directed.

   B. Only some of the foreign entries were brilliantly directed.

10. Only the documentaries, which proved to be disappointing this year, represented a poor selection.

    A. The documentaries in general were a poor selection.

    B. Only some of the documentaries were a poor selection.

11. We hope to see further works from the new entrants from the African countries whose film industries are just emerging.

    A. The film industries in African countries in general are just emerging.

    B. The film industries in some African countries are just emerging.

12. If such excellence in selection and presentation continues, the Moonrise Film Festival will soon take its place among the film festivals of the world that rival Cannes.

    A. Film festivals in general rival Cannes.

    B. Only some film festivals rival Cannes.

5. Editing

In the following article, find and correct the eighteen errors in the formation of the adjective clauses.

One of the ways in ~~whom~~ *in which* people can be classified is by labeling them extroverts and introverts. However, there are other methods, some of them are now considered to have little scientific value, that people use to conveniently pigeonhole members of the human race.

For example, there is the division into mesomorphs, who are muscular; endomorphs, who tend to be fat; and ectomorphs, who are thin. The endomorph is stereotyped as a relaxed and unobsessive personality, whereas the ectomorph is stereotyped as a person whom is nervous and serious and whom rarely smiles.

A further facile division is made by defining people as Type A and Type B. Type A describes people to which everything is serious and who they are very ambitious and driving. Type A originally described people, usually middle-aged males, whom often suffered heart attacks. Type B, on the other hand, labels a rather passive, ambitionless person of that others frequently take advantage, and which is probably not a candidate for a heart attack.

Some people categorize human beings by the astrological sign that they were born under it. For example, a person who born between April 22 and May 21 is called a Taurus and is supposed to possess certain characteristics such as congeniality and tact. A person that born between June 22 and July 21 is a Cancer and is reputed to be stubborn but effective. There are twelve such categories, which encompass all the months of the year. Many people base their lives and relationships on the predictions made by astrologers.

One recent theory to categorize people is the theory of left-brained and right-brained people. Right-brained people, that are intuitive and romantic, are the artists and creative people of the world according to this theory. Left-brained people, who they are logical in their thinking, turn out to be mathematicians and scientists. According to this theory, people whose their functioning is not developed enough in the areas they would like can act to develop the side of the brain they want to improve it in order to better balance their personality.

All of these theories, which in themselves are too simplistic, are indeed unscientific. However, they have provided attractive and sometimes amusing solutions for people are looking for easy ways to understand the human race. Different theories of categorizing people, which it is always a difficult thing to do, will continue to come and go.

6. Personalization

Write a description of the kind of person you would like to marry. If you are married, pretend you are not and describe an imaginary ideal person. Include some of the phrases in the box, appropriately finished with adjective clauses.

> I'd like to marry a person who . . .
>
> This will be a person whom . . .
>
> My ideal person will be someone whose . . .
>
> We will have a marriage that . . .
>
> We will have a home we . . .
>
> I look forward to a wonderful life with my husband/wife, who . . .

UNIT 17
Adjective Clauses with Quantifiers; Adjectival Modifying Phrases

1. Identifying Adjective Clauses and Adjective Phrases

In the following passage, underline the adjective clauses and circle the adjective phrases.

The movie industry, (barely born before the turn of the century,) began producing silent films in the early 1900s. Filmmakers, learning how to fake prizefights, news events, and foreign settings, increased the length and variety of their films. Some of the early filmmakers, however, actually provided coverage of certain news events, <u>among which were the inauguration of President William McKinley and the action at the front in the Boer War</u>. Travelogues, many of which were filmed in remote parts of the world, became very popular, as did short science films, made with the aid of the microscope.

One of the important technical film pioneers was French magician Georges Méliès, credited with creating methods leading toward the development of special-effects movies. He used innovative techniques, examples of which include double exposure, mattes, slow and fast motion, animation, and miniature models. Through these techniques, he was able to create popular film fantasies, one of which was called *A Trip to the Moon* and influenced many subsequent filmmakers.

At the same time, filmmakers in England were developing fiction films shot outdoors, some of which involved chase scenes. In 1903, Edwin S. Porter, a camera operator and director, made *The Great Train Robbery,* a movie showing different actions simultaneously. For some chase scenes, Porter mounted a camera in a car of a train. Along with bringing excitement and suspense to the movies, Porter firmly established the genre of the chase film, seen and loved even today.

Thus began the era of the silent film, changing the world forever.

2. Forming Adjective Clauses with Quantifiers

The following sentences present some interesting facts.* Complete these sentences by writing adjective clauses with quantifiers (or other expressions of quantity) + preposition + relative pronoun.

1. The average American's diet contains quite a bit of sodium, *most of which comes from processed food*.
   (most / come / from processed food)

2. In the past 20 years in Florida, insects, spiders, and alligators have caused 82 deaths, _____.
   (most / could / have / be avoided)

3. Hospital stays in Japan, _____, are far longer than hospital stays in the United States.
   (half / be / longer than / 40 days)

4. According to survey results, Americans today, _____, feel more victimized than did Americans in the past.
   (71 percent / think / people in power take advantage of others)

5. According to intelligence test results, stutterers, _____, appear to be smarter than nonstutterers.
   (14 percent / achieve scores of over 130 on IQ tests)

6. The hearing impaired, _____, are a more diverse group than is sometimes thought.
   (more than half / be / under 64 years old)

7. Vegetables, _____, can be microwaved, stir-fried, or quick-steamed.
   (all / yield / more nutrients when lightly cooked than when raw)

8. Americans eat an average of 21.5 pounds per year of food between meals, _____.
   (much / be / junk food)

* The information is taken from *Health,* October 1993 and November–December 1994.

3. Reducing Adjective Clauses to Adjective Phrases

Read the following descriptions of movies from a publication for TV viewers. Change the adjective clauses in parentheses to adjective phrases.

1. ROCKY II
In the sequel to the 1976 blockbuster, heavyweight Rocky Balboa gets a rematch in this action thriller, *written and directed by and again starring Sylvester Stallone*.
(which was written and directed by and again stars Sylvester Stallone)

2. INDOCHINE
This is an Oscar-winning chronicle of French colonialism, _____.
(which is embodied by Catherine Deneuve as a plantation owner)

ADJECTIVE CLAUSES WITH QUANTIFIERS; ADJECTIVAL MODIFYING PHRASES ▼ 115

3. JEZEBEL
Bette Davis won an Oscar for her portrayal of a pre–Civil War southern vixen who causes problems for the unfortunate people _____
(who surround her)
_____.

4. BEAUTY AND THE BEAST
This superlative animated musical from Disney tells of the romance between a beautiful young girl and a prince _____
(who has been transformed by a magic spell)
_____.

5. THE BIG CHILL
Fine ensemble acting distinguishes Lawrence Kasdan's story of college friends _____
_____.
(who have been reunited for a funeral)

6. BORN FREE
This is a touching, fact-based heartwarmer about a couple _____
(who is raising a lion cub in Kenya)
_____.

7. DAVE
Kevin Kline plays a dual role in this political satire about an employment agency owner _____
(who has been enlisted to impersonate the president of the United States)
_____.

8. FAR AND AWAY
Tom Cruise and Nicole Kidman play an Irish tenant farmer and a landowner's feisty daughter, _____
(who fall into trouble as they immigrate to America)
_____.

9. FREE WILLY
An orphan befriends a neglected killer whale _____
(which is held in captivity)
_____.

10. GORILLAS IN THE MIST
Sigourney Weaver portrays naturalist Dian Fossey, _____
(who fought to save Africa's gorillas from extinction)
_____.

11. HOME ALONE 2
This sequel finds Kevin, _____
(who is again separated from his vacationing family)
and _____, in various adventures.
(who faces similar woes)

12. HOWARDS END
This is an adaptation of E.M. Forster's Edwardian novel about two British sisters _____
_____.
(who become involved with a wealthy family)

4. Adjective Clauses with Quantifiers and Using Adjective Phrases

Read the following pairs of sentences. For each pair of sentences, combine the second sentence with the first one. Use an adjective phrase or, if the second sentence has a quantifier, an adjective clause with a quantifier.

If you are going to buy a computer, you must be aware of several things.

1. First, there are two basic types of personal computers. These two types of personal computers are the IBM (or IBM-compatible) and the Macintosh.

    First, there are two basic types of personal computers, the IBM (or IBM-compatible) and the Macintosh.

2. Then, there are various places where you can buy computers. These places include computer stores, electronics stores, office-supply stores, and mail-order houses.

3. At reasonable prices you can get everything you need. The prices range from $1,200 to $3,000.

4. Within this price range, of course, you will find varying capabilities among the computers. Many of the computers come equipped with a fax/modem.

5. Many major brands of computer have a toll-free number. This number is given to customers so that they may call the company for technical assistance.

6. If you are a new buyer, you should buy from a store where you know you can get help. A new buyer has little experience with computers.

7. While you are shopping around, you will find words like *hard drive*, *megabyte*, and *CD-ROM drive*. These words are all part of a computer owner's vocabulary.

8. If you need your computer while you are traveling, you should consider a laptop. A laptop is small enough and light enough to carry with you.

9. Sometimes computers come with programs. The programs have already been installed at the factory.

10. You don't have to buy many extra capabilities right away. The capabilities are unneeded by beginners.

11. For newcomers to computers, it's a good idea to take some classes or to get a tutor. Both of these can usually be arranged by the store.

5. Editing

Read the following passage on films after World War II. Find and correct the fifteen errors involving adjective clauses and phrases. Delete, fix, or replace words, but do not change punctuation or add words.

After World War II, Europe was the center of important developments in filmmaking, which ~~they~~ strongly influenced motion pictures worldwide. In Italy, well-known movies, some of them were Rossellini's *Open City,* making in 1945, and De Sica's *Shoeshine* (1946) and *Bicycle Thief* (1948), established a trend toward realism in film. These directors weren't concerned with contrived plots or stories that produced for entertainment value alone; they took their cameras into the streets to make films showed the harshness of life in the years after the war. In the next decades, Federico Fellini, was an outstanding director, combined realistic plots with poetic imagery, symbolism, and philosophical ideas in now-classic films, the most famous of them is *La Strada,* which a movie ostensibly about circus people in the streets but really about the meaning of life.

In France, a group of young filmmakers, calling the "New Wave," appeared during the 1950s.

(continued on next page)

This group developed a new kind of focus, which stressed characterization rather than plot, and new camera and acting techniques, seeing in movies such as Truffaut's *400 Blows*. In England, another group of filmmakers, was known as the "Angry Young Man" movement, developed a new realism. In Sweden, Ingmar Bergman used simple stories and allegories to look at complex philosophical and social issues, some of them are masterfully explored in *The Seventh Seal*. The Spaniard Luis Buñuel depicted social injustices and used surrealistic techniques, creating films like *Viridiana*.

Postwar developments in filmmaking were not limited to Western Europe. The Japanese director Akira Kurosawa, was the first Asian filmmaker to have a significant influence in Europe, made *Rashomon* in 1950. Movies from India, like Satyajit Ray's *Pather Panchali,* showed us life on the subcontinent. Even in Russia, where filmmaking was under state control, it was possible to make movies like *The Cranes Are Flying,* portray the problems of the individual. Russian directors also made films based on literary classics, included Shakespeare's plays and Tolstoi's monumental historical novel, *War and Peace*.

In summary, in the decades after World War II, filmmaking turned in new directions, as shown by a wide range of movies from around the world, many of them focused on the meaning of life and how to interpret it.

6. Personalization

What was the best movie that you have ever seen? What can you remember about it? Write a short essay about the movie. Begin with this sentence: **One of my favorite movies is _____**. Include some of the phrases in the boxes.

> I liked the movie for a number of reasons, some of which are . . .
>
> The movie had some good actors, including . . .
>
> The movie had some really exciting (funny) scenes, examples of which are . . .
>
> I remember the scene taking place . . .
>
> There was an exciting plot, involving . . .
>
> The movie had an interesting ending, resulting in . . .

The director was _____, also known for directing . . .

I like his (her) movies, all of which . . .

The movie won some awards, including . . .

I would have no trouble recommending this movie, one of the . . .

Perhaps this movie will be shown again soon, in which case . . .

UNIT 18

PART VII: NOUN CLAUSES

Noun Clauses: Subjects and Objects

1. Identifying Noun Clauses

Read the following from an organization that promotes peace. Underline the noun clauses.

"There is many a boy here today who looks on war as glory, but boys, it is all hell." Are these words the words of a pacifist, of a conscientious objector, who believes <u>that wars should not be fought by people who don't believe in war</u>? No, this is an utterance by General William Tecumseh Sherman, a Union general in the American Civil War, who is remembered for his devastating march through the American South, and who had often stated unequivocally that ruthlessness in modern war is necessary.

Who fights in wars? Who thinks that sacrificing one's life and the lives of others is glorious? While many enter the service as a career, or with patriotic zeal during a war, many more are conscripted by their governments. This means compulsory enrollment in the armed forces, in war or in peace. That all a nation's able-bodied men give compulsory military service was an idea introduced in the late eighteenth century during the French Revolution; it enabled Napoleon, several years later, to raise huge armies. This kind of system, in which the government conscripted whoever was able, was adopted by other European countries during the nineteenth century. What took place in the United States was wartime conscription during the Civil War and in both world wars, as well as a draft maintained from 1945 to 1973.

Our organization asks why people go to war. We question whether any territorial imperative, commercial advantage, or religious belief can justify the loss of even one life. And because war is wrong, we must do whatever we can to end conscription everywhere. We firmly maintain that no cause, however just, is rationale enough to force a man to fight to kill.

2. Using Noun Clauses as Subjects

In this conversation, complete the answers by forming noun clauses based on the questions.

A: What did the boss tell Charlie?

B: *What the boss told Charlie* does not concern me.
                 1.

A: Who talked to the boss about Charlie?

B: _____ is none of my business.
                 2.

A: Where is Charlie now?

B: _____ is not my concern.
                 3.

A: When is Charlie going to be arrested?

B: _____ does not interest me.
                 4.

A: When was the money stolen?

B: _____ doesn't matter at this point.
                 5.

A: What will happen to Charlie?

B: _____ is no concern of mine.
                 6.

A: I wonder whether or not Charlie is a thief.

B: I don't. _____ won't change the world.
                         7.

A: It's amazing! We have a big-time embezzler in our company!

B: The fact that _____ hasn't been established yet.
                               8.

A: I don't understand. What do you think about this news?

B: I thought you understood by now. _____ is that it's not right to gossip.
                                           9.

3. Using Noun Clauses as Objects

Beth Crier, a reporter on a high school newspaper, has interviewed Mr. Fred Evans, the director of sports at her school. Complete his answers by forming noun clauses based on the questions. Introduce each clause with one of the following words: **what, where, that, whatever, whoever.**

Crier: Are sports important to the development of young people?

Evans: Yes, anyone involved with young people and sports can tell you *that sports are*
                                                                                       1.
important to the development of young people.

(continued on next page)

Crier: In that case, do you think a school's curriculum should include a strong sports program?

Evans: Definitely. I'm firmly convinced _____
2.
_____.

Crier: What can students do to become part of a team?

Evans: I'm often asked _____
3.
_____. The first step, of course, is to come and try out for the team.

Crier: I've heard that in order to be on a team students don't have to have a lot of talent. Is this true? Can anyone who is interested in a sport and tries hard be on a team?

Evans: Absolutely. There's a place on a team for _____
4.
_____.

Crier: Is training necessary?

Evans: Yes. And prospective team members should be prepared to do _____
5.
_____.

Crier: Is the training difficult?

Evans: Sometimes it can be. But anyone who is really committed to a team doesn't care _____
6.
_____.

Crier: Tell me how it works for an individual student on the team. What does he or she have to do? Where does he or she belong?

Evans: It's hard to give a general answer to those questions. But I can assure you that before long each student on a team knows _____
7.
and _____.
8.

Crier: What does it feel like to be a team player?

Evans: The players don't usually talk about _____,
9.
_____, but it's obvious that they feel good about themselves.

4. Editing

Read the following passage. Find and correct the nine errors in the use of noun clauses.

Among conscientious objectors are the Quakers, also known as the Religious Society of Friends. The Quaker religion originated in seventeenth-century England with George Fox, who believed ~~what~~ *that* a person needs no spiritual intermediary. He sought to know how does a person find understanding and guidance and concluded that is it through an "inward light," supplied by the Holy Spirit. The early Quakers refused to attend the Church of England services or to pay tithes to the church. They questioned what were the real values in life, and they were frugal and plain in their dress and speech. In those times, whomever opposed the customs of the established church was persecuted. Thus, the Quakers met with fines, confiscation of property, and even imprisonment. Some emigrated to Asia and Africa, but particularly to America, where they found refuge in Rhode Island and in Pennsylvania, a colony established in 1682 by William Penn, who was himself a Quaker.

Quakers do not believe in taking part in war because they feel that war it causes spiritual damage through hatred. Most Quakers refuse to serve in the military, although individuals can follow whatever convictions do they personally hold. Because their resistance is based on religious and humanitarian convictions, the U.S. and British governments have allowed them to substitute nonmilitary service for that would normally be a military service requirement.

Quaker meetings are periods of silent meditation, where members speak if they are urged by the spirit. Quakers are active in education and social welfare. They believe society should treat all its citizens as equals. The American Friends Service Committee organizes relief and service projects for whatever in the world help is needed.

5. Personalization

Have you ever pondered the meaning of life? Describe some of the things you have thought about. Include some of the partial sentences in the box.

> I've often wondered what life . . .
>
> I've sometimes thought that . . .
>
> That a higher force exists seems . . .
>
> I really don't understand how . . .
>
> What life's meaning is seems . . .
>
> I have sometimes asked whether it . . .
>
> Nobody has been able to tell me if there . . .
>
> Perhaps one day I will comprehend why . . .
>
> I am convinced that . . .

_____

_____

_____

_____

_____

_____

_____

_____

_____

_____

_____

_____

_____

1. Identifying Adjective and Subject Complements

Underline the ten noun clauses that are used as adjective complements or subject complements. Label the clauses as adjective complement or subject complement.

THE SUNDAY MAGAZINE

By now, much has been made of gender differences in language. Partly because of the recent publication of several books and articles on the subject, it appears clear to many people <u>that men speak more directly than women do</u> [*adjective complement*] and, in addition, that a direct way of speaking is more effective than an indirect way of speaking. It is also a sign of power and self-confidence. ("Type this letter" or "Could you please type this letter" are examples of direct ways of speaking. In contrast, "This letter needs to be typed right away" is an example of an indirect way of conveying the same message.)

However, Dr. Deborah Tannen, a linguist who is an expert in speech patterns, questions these commonly held beliefs. "I challenge the assumption that talking in an indirect way necessarily reveals powerlessness, lack of self-confidence, or anything else about the character of the speaker," she says in an article in the *New York Times*. Moreover, a key finding of hers is that the degree of directness of speech varies greatly among cultures. Finally, according to Tannen, it is also likely that both women and men are indirect. They are often just indirect in different ways, she says.

Addressing the question of effectiveness in giving commands, she does not think it is true that

(continued on next page)

directness always works best. On the contrary, indirectness is often appropriate and successful. She cites examples from the army and from business offices, in which the boss, or the higher-ranking person, effectively uses very indirectly stated orders. For instance, the high-ranking person says: "It's cold in here." These words are really an indirect order; that is, the person's expectation is that one of the subordinates will close the window right away. Or the high-ranking person says, "I wonder whether there is information available on this subject." When these words are spoken, it is advisable that the subordinate quickly find and present the information. Because everybody understands who is in charge, the indirect way of speaking works well.

It should appear obvious, then, that more than the choice of vocabulary and tone of voice determine whether a command is successful. Indeed, a very important consideration is that the status of the speaker and the listener be mutually understood and that both people interact in accordance with the unwritten rules of this understanding. Both women and men can issue effective commands, and both indirect and direct ways of speaking can be effective.

2. Writing Adjective, Subject, and Verb Complements

Complete the following letter by filling in blanks with the indicated words to form appropriate adjective, subject, and verb complements. Include the word **that**. Write noun clauses, although a few of the sentences could also be completed in other ways.

Dear Ricardo,

I got your letter. You are really direct, and you are also right. It's true _that I have to shape up_.
1. (I / have to / shape up)

I know it's essential _____. Yet it also seems clear _____.
2. (I / forget / about Lisa)   3. (this / be / much easier said than done)

The problem is _____. I'm sure that you're right when you say that somebody
4. (I / not / can / forget / about her)

new might make me forget. But the big difficulty with this is _____. I'm
5. (I / not / be / receptive to meeting people)

going to try, though. My goal now is _____.
6. (I / get / my life in order)

And you, Ricardo—what's going to happen to you? You lost another job! It's absolutely

necessary _____. It's obvious _____.
         7. (you / be / responsible on the job)   8. (you / have / always / be / too casual about your work)

It's vital _____, if you get one. I recommend _____.
          9. (you / keep / the next job / you / get)   10. (you / adopt / a better attitude)

And I strongly suggest _____.
                       11. (you / not / invest / any more money in bad deals)

With that advice, I'm signing off.

Marco

3. Using Noun Clauses as Adjective Complements

Read the following proverbs. Write paraphrases of the proverbs by using the cues to write sentences in the form **It is** + *adjective* + *noun clause with* **that.** *Then match the paraphrases to the proverbs by putting the correct letter after each paraphrase.*

A. All work and no play makes Jack a dull boy.

B. A stitch in time saves nine.

C. Rome wasn't built in a day.

D. The early bird gets the worm.

E. Children should be seen and not heard.

F. People who live in glass houses shouldn't throw stones.

G. A bird in the hand is worth two in the bush.

H. Don't put the cart before the horse.

I. Don't cry over spilt milk.

J. There's no use putting a lock on the barn door after the horse has been stolen.

1. ___E. *It is advisable that children be seen and not heard.*___
      advisable / children / be / see / and not / hear

2. _____
      necessary / time / be / take / to do a job right

3. _____
      advisable / you / not criticize / others because you have faults, too

4. _____
      essential / things / be / do / in the right order

5. _____
      advisable / problems / be / take care of / before they get worse

6. _____
      important / you / not be upset / over what already happened

(continued on next page)

7. _____
   desirable / a person / stick / with what he or she already has rather than going after other things

8. _____
   vital / a person / enjoy life / as well as / work

9. _____
   essential / a person / get / an early start to beat the competition

10. _____
    necessary / precautions / be / take / *before* there is trouble.

4. Editing

Read the following essay. Find and correct the eight errors related to noun clauses. Several noun clauses are used correctly.

Would you believe that listening to the music of Mozart actually makes you smarter? According to a study, ^it is true that Mozart's music has this effect! Recently, researchers at the University of California, Irvine, found that the IQ scores of college students went up nine points after the students had been listening to Mozart for ten minutes. In another experiment, it appeared that Mozart's music helped students to solve spatial puzzles involving cutout shapes. The fact it is that students who listened to Mozart performed better than those who listened to another composer's music.

These research findings lead to some fascinating speculations. If it is clear that experiencing Mozart raise the level of intelligence, shouldn't we all have his music on at every moment? Shouldn't we be using our Walkmans at the office, playing tapes of Mozart's music while we work?

That a schoolchild studying multiplication tables should play Mozart in the background it seems clear. The child should not listen to Sibelius or Bach, and certainly should not listen to rock or rap. It should be obvious to the parents because that they must fill the house with Mozart's music and insist that the child listen to Mozart and only Mozart when studying. What's more, parents should demand the child listen to Mozart on a headset while playing competitive sports. Of course, the problem is that as soon as parents begin to insist that something is done in a certain way, they will meet strong resistance from their children.

Another obvious problem is it that much more research must be done before we can believe that Mozart's music can actually make you smarter. Meanwhile, though, I personally am willing to try anything, especially the pleasant task of immersing myself in beautiful music! *

* Based on "Classic View," by Alex Ross, *The New York Times,* August 28, 1994.

5. Personalization

What do you think is necessary to improve the quality of education in today's world? Answer this question in a short essay. Include some of the phrases in the box.

> A main problem in education is the fact that . . .
>
> A main problem in our schools is that . . .
>
> It is known that . . .
>
> That schools should . . . is clear.
>
> That students need . . . is obvious.
>
> It is absolutely essential that . . .
>
> It is also desirable that . . .
>
> I would recommend that . . .
>
> We must insist that . . .
>
> The result of making changes like these will be that . . .

UNIT 20: Unreal Conditionals and Other Ways to Express Unreality

PART VIII: UNREAL CONDITIONS

1. Identifying Unreal Conditionals

Read the following. Underline the unreal conditionals. Do not underline real conditionals.

The dictionary defines "chocoholic" as a person who has a near obsession for chocolate. The world is full of chocoholics. Yet, <u>if it hadn't been for an unusual sequence of events, these people would probably never have tasted chocolate</u>.

Until the Spanish explorers brought chocolate back from the New World, it was totally unknown in Europe. Arriving in Mexico in the early 1500s, Hernán Cortés discovered that the Indians there drank a delicious, dark, frothy beverage called *chocolatl*, brewed from the beans of the native cacao plant. Cacao beans were so highly valued in the area that they were used as currency. In the marketplace of Chichén Itzá, a center of Mayan Indian civilization, four beans would buy a pumpkin and 100 would buy a slave. The Indians of Mexico evidently had chocoholics as well as chocolate. Whenever the Aztec Indian king Montezuma didn't drink his 50 pitchers of *chocolatl* a day, it is said, he would feel a strong physical need for it.

It's a good thing for the chocolate lovers of the world that Cortés actually met Montezuma. If he hadn't, the delicious substance might never have crossed the ocean to Spain. Chocolate was popular in Spain for a century before the news of its divine taste and reputed medicinal and psychological powers spread to other European countries. In mid-seventeenth-century London, chocolate houses, like coffee houses, sprang up; only the aristocrats could enjoy the drink, however, because of its high cost. If it hadn't been so expensive, the masses could have enjoyed it much sooner.

Theobromine, a substance similar to caffeine, is found in chocolate, which explains why people felt energized after drinking chocolate. Doctors of the era reported that chocolate was an effective medicine, imparting energy, among other things. If people wanted to feel stronger fast, they could imbibe some of the drink.

Chocolate was primarily a beverage until the 1800s, when a Swiss chocolatier combined chocolate with milk solids. If this chocolatier hadn't, we would not have the wide range of candies and candy bars that we have today. If he hadn't, Switzerland and the Netherlands would not have become the great producers of quality chocolates that they are. Last but not least, if he hadn't, we would not have chocolate cakes or chocolate chip cookies.

Today, 75 percent of the cacao comes from Africa, and the rest comes from Central America, Ecuador, and Brazil. Chocolate is consumed all over the world, but particularly in Western Europe and in the United States. Clearly, if there were not such a well-developed world trade, chocolate lovers would not be able to indulge themselves so easily.

But, chocolate does have some bad effects. It contains a lot of fats and sugar, so if people eat too much, they can develop or worsen conditions such as hardening of the arteries or diabetes. Doctors and dentists have been telling patients for a long time that if their fat and sugar intake were lower, they would be healthier. Such warnings do not do much to inhibit chocoholics. Says one chocoholic, "Quite frankly, if I had a day without chocolate, it would be like a day without sunshine." *

* Information taken from Richard B. Manchester, *Amazing Facts,* (New York: Bristol Park Books, 1991).

2. Relating Unreal Conditions to Real Conditions

The following sentences express unreal conditions. After these sentences, write sentences that express what the real conditions are.

1. If chocolate weren't so delicious, people wouldn't crave it.

   Chocolate ___is delicious_____.

   People ___crave it_____.

2. If chocolate hadn't been brought back to Europe by the Spanish explorers, it might not be popular today.

   Chocolate _____.

   It _____.

(continued on next page)

3. People would be healthy if they didn't eat a lot of chocolate and other foods containing fat and sugar.

People _____.

They _____.

4. If people ate a balanced diet, they would be well nourished.

People _____.

They _____.

5. Some people wish that they had enough willpower to refuse junk food.

Some people don't _____.

6. People on diets often wish, for example, that they hadn't consumed 4,000 calories at the last meal that they ate.

Some people on diets actually _____.

7. Gourmands are people who eat greedily, as though there were no tomorrow.

There really _____.

8. If only dieting were easy!

Dieting _____.

3. Expressing Conditions in the Present Time

Complete Jane's diary. In the first four paragraphs, fill in the blanks with appropriate clauses expressing unreal conditions *in the present time. Use* **would** *in conditional sentences. In the last paragraph, fill in the blanks with clauses expressing* possible conditions *in the present time.*

Dear Diary,

   I have just come from Cousin Hattie's annual Thanksgiving dinner, where once again I had to endure all the questions from family members about why I am not married.

   This really upsets me! I'm not married because I choose not to be. If _I chose to be married, I would be married_. Actually, part of the reason is that I never meet
   1. (I / choose / be married / I / be married)
anyone I really like. Perhaps, if_____.
                              2. (I / meet / the right man / I / have a different feeling about it)
   As usual, everyone was worried about me, thinking that I'm lonely. If

_____. But I do have a lot of friends, so I'm fine.
　　　　3. (I / not have / a lot of friends / I / be lonely)

Maybe if _____. But I like my job a lot.
　　　　　　4. (I / not like / my job / I / be unhappy)

I'm tired of being nagged about the subject of marriage all the time. I really wish

_____. My family sometimes treats me as though
　　5. (people / leave / me alone)

_____ for choosing to remain single. But I am not weird.
　　6. (I / be / a / weird person)

Actually, I wouldn't mind having a partner in life. If only

_____! Not to sound greedy, but sometimes I wish
　　7. (I / can / meet / the perfect man tomorrow)

_____ —a successful career, travel, an active social
　　8. (I / have / it all)

life, and a husband and children. I think I could manage it.

　　　Actually, I do hope _____ really nice. But where? I know! I'll
　　　　　　　　　　　　　　9. (I / meet / somebody)

try Warm Hearts. From what I've heard, it seems as if _____.
　　　　　　　　　　　　　　　　　　　　　　　　10. (that / be / an excellent matchmaking service)

If only _____! Then what will my family nag
　　　　11. (they / introduce / me to someone perfect)

me about?

4. Expressing Conditionals in the Past Time

*Complete the letter by filling in the blanks to express unreal conditions in the past time. Use the indicated words, and use **would** in the result clauses of conditional sentences.*

Dear Ricardo,

　　Well, all's well that ends well, as Shakespeare said. Even though a lot of bad things happened to me, my year here in the United States has actually been pretty good. First, and most important, I met Suzie. It's a good thing, because if I ____*hadn't met*____ Suzie, I would have been suffering
　　　　　　　　　　　　　　　　　　　　　　1. (meet / not)
over Lisa for a really long time. For that matter, it's a good thing that I had the automobile accident; if I hadn't crashed into that little blue Mazda, I _____ its driver, who turned out
　　　　　　　　　　　　　　　　　　　　　　　2. (never / meet)

(continued on next page)

to be Suzie. Suzie has taken over my life, and it's so much better now. Suzie influenced me to drop my history course. I didn't know that it was possible to drop courses. If I hadn't dropped the course, I _____ (3. fail) it for sure. I wish that I _____ (4. not / waste) so much time taking it; I should have dropped it sooner. Another thing that's much better since I met Suzie: the food. Yes, Suzie is a wonderful cook. If I had known Suzie earlier, I _____ (5. not / have to eat) all those terrible meals at the beginning of the semester. If I had known Suzie earlier, I _____ (6. know) where to get an apartment and where to shop. If I had known Suzie earlier, I _____ (7. not / be) as lonesome and homesick as I was at the beginning, and I certainly _____ (8. not / suffer) over Lisa like a stupid, lovesick puppy the way that I did. If only I _____ (9. meet) her when I first came here!

I'm glad that you're OK now, too, Ricardo. It's too bad that things didn't work out at the hotel. Maybe if you _____ (10. not / fall asleep) at the desk so often at that job, you wouldn't have gotten fired. But as my mother always says, "Things work out for the best," and your present job making movies sounds glamorous. Just think, if you hadn't gotten fired, you _____ (11. not / be able to) take the job with the movie producer last spring. And, taking classes at night and working during the day is a good idea. Who knows? Maybe you'll even become a movie star. Of course, you might become very snobbish as a movie star and act as though you _____ (12. never / meet) me or anybody else from our childhood. But I think that won't happen.

Actually, I wish that the bad stuff this year _____ (13. not / happen), but as I said, everything's turning out OK. You have a great and glamorous new job, you're paying off your debts and you have a future. I will finish school here, and I have a wonderful new girlfriend. If we _____ (14. not / make) some of the mistakes we did, these good things _____ (15. pass) us by. What you should do is visit me here in the United States when you are between movies, or maybe when you come to the United States "on location."

See you soon, I hope.

Marco

5. Editing

Read the following letter. Find and correct the nine errors in the forms of the verbs in the conditional and related sentences.

Dear Elinor,

I am writing because I want to talk to you about a woman I met though Warm Hearts, a matchmaking service here in Beautiville. Her name is Jane, and I'd like to build a relationship with her. The trouble is that I'm too shy. Oh, I wish I ~~didn't be~~ *weren't* so shy! If I weren't so shy, I would called her up to invite her out to dinner. It's a good thing that I signed up with Warm Hearts. If I hadn't, I would never had met such a wonderful girl, because as you know, I just can't bring myself to call anyone for a date.

Anyway, Jane is beautiful and smart and very nice. I think I am falling in love with her, and I haven't even spent time with her. We've only talked on the phone. I wish we have already been out together a hundred times. I feel as though I knew her all my life. If you talked to her, you would liked her, too, I know.

Elinor, here's my question. You know I have always been a shy man. If I actually gathered enough courage to ask her out, what did she say? I think she'd say yes, because, after all, she joined the dating service and she does spend time with me on the phone. It isn't as though we are kids, either. She's 40, just a few years younger than I am. So, Elinor, what do you think I should do?

I hope that you answered me soon.

Your brother Gus

6. Personalization

How would you evaluate the quality of your life at this point? Have you made decisions which turned out well? Write a short essay about your life now and about how decisions you made have influenced your life. Finish some of the sentences in the box.

> The best decision I have made in my life was . . .
>
> If I had made the opposite decision, . . .
>
> On the other hand, a bad decision was . . .
>
> I wish I . . .
>
> If I . . .
>
> There are many aspects of my present situation that I wouldn't change. For example, I wouldn't change . . .
>
> If I were to change . . .
>
> My life now is too . . .
>
> I wish my life . . .
>
> If my life . . .
>
> I hope . . .

Unit 21: Inverted and Implied Conditionals; Subjunctive in Noun Clauses

1. Identifying Inverted and Implied Conditionals and Subjunctives in Noun Clauses

In the following article,* look for inverted and implied conditionals and subjunctives in noun clauses. Underline clauses containing an inverted conditional (do not underline other conditional clauses), words introducing implied conditionals, and verbs in subjunctive form in noun clauses.

It is difficult to imagine what life would be like today <u>had the can opener not been invented</u>. Without the simple little tool that we take for granted, how would we open cans? It is essential that we have the can opener to gain the enormous advantages in time, variety of foods, and, most of all, convenience that the use of canned goods gives us. What if we had no way of preserving the foods we are so accustomed to buying in cans today? We would not be eating the tuna, canned hams, or out-of-season peas and peaches that are so much a part of our lifestyle. Without canned tuna, the popular tuna sandwich wouldn't exist.

Interestingly, metal cans to preserve food had been in existence for a full fifty years before a device similar to the can opener we know today was invented. Developed in England in 1810, the first "tin canisters" were actually made of iron and sometimes heavier than the food they contained. British soldiers in the War of 1812 opened canned rations with bayonets, knives, or even rifles. On an Arctic expedition in 1824, British explorer Sir William Parry took along a can of veal, the instructions of which read: "Cut round on the top with a chisel and hammer"; empty, the can weighed more than a pound. By the 1850s, cans were made of a lighter metal and had a rim around the top. Around this time, Ezra J. Warner of Waterbury, Connecticut, devised a "can opener." This opener was part bayonet and part sickle; if not used correctly, it could be lethal. Had the U.S. military not adopted this primitive can opener in the Civil War, surely the unwieldy invention would soon have become extinct.

But, as the saying has it, necessity is the mother of invention. In 1870, William J. Lyman patented a device that was revolutionary in concept and design: it had a cutting wheel that rolled around the rim of the can. Because of the ease with which cans could now be opened, by 1895 canned goods were a familiar sight on grocery store shelves. In 1925 a serrated rotation wheel was added, and in 1931 the electric can opener was introduced.

The evolution of this important invention did not occur overnight. How fortunate we are that lightweight cans and easy-to-use can openers were invented; otherwise, we would not have the convenience and variety in foods that we have.

---

* Based on Charles Panati, *Extraordinary Origins of Everyday Things,* (Perennial Library, Harper & Row, 1987, Revised 1989).

2. Using the Subjunctive in Noun Clauses

In the following material providing advice to travelers, incorporate each sentence in parentheses into the next sentence as a noun clause.

1. (A driver must keep to the right-hand side of the road.)

    In the United States and many European countries, it is essential *that a driver keep to the right-hand side of the road*.

2. (He or she has to drive on the left.)

    In Japan and England, however, it is mandatory _____
    _____.

3. (People should remove their shoes before going inside a house.)

    In some places, such as Japan and Saudi Arabia, it is important _____
    _____.

4. (People should keep their shoes on.)

    In other places, it is expected _____
    _____.

5. (People must not eat pork products.)

    In some places, religious laws demand _____
    _____.

6. (Pork products must be avoided.)

    This is because in olden times, the hot weather required _____
    _____, because of the strong possibility of food contamination.

7. (A sick person should take vitamin C.)

    In some places, doctors recommend _____
    _____.

8. (A sick person should have a lot of homemade chicken soup.)

    In other places, they advise _____
    _____.

9. (A waiter should be summoned by whistling.)

    In some places, it is suggested _____
    _____.

(continued on next page)

10. (A waiter must not be summoned by whistling.)

   In other places, it is recommended _____

   _____, because this would be considered exceedingly rude.

11. (A traveler ought to learn about customs in various places.)

   Logic suggests _____

   _____.

3. Using Inverted and Implied Conditionals in the Past Time

Complete the following answers to questions in an American history examination by filling in the blanks with the appropriate conditional forms of the verbs indicated. Use **would** *in result clauses unless another auxiliary is indicated.*

1. As everyone knows, Columbus discovered the New World quite accidentally while searching for a shorter route to India. Had he __*not been searching*__ (not / be searching) for that shorter route to India, he __*would not have discovered*__ (not / discover) the New World.

2. The American colonists formally gained their independence from England in 1783. Had the Americans _____ (not / gain) their independence from England, America _____ (remain) a British colony.

3. In the American Civil War, fought from 1861 to 1865, the North had greater resources and finally won the war. Without these resources, the North _____ (might / not / win) the Civil War.

4. The railroads were very important to the development of the American West and directly contributed to the growth of California. Without the railroads, California _____ (not / grow) as quickly as it did.

5. During its history, America has attracted and welcomed people from many different cultures. Had America _____ (reject) these differing peoples, the country _____ (not / become) the multicultural nation that it is today.

6. Women won the right to vote in the United States in 1920. Had women _____ (not / win) that right in 1920, it is probable that they _____ (gain) it before now in any case.

7. In 1955, Jonas Salk, an American physician, developed a vaccine to prevent polio. It is indeed fortunate that he developed this vaccine; if not, many more people _____ (die) of polio in the last forty years.

8. John F. Kennedy was assassinated in November 1963. Had he _____ (live), he probably _____ (serve) two terms as president of the United States.

4. Writing Conditionals

*For each of the following sentences, write a corresponding conditional sentence that expresses the opposite situation. Begin the sentence with the phrase given and include **would** or **wouldn't**.*

How do major inventions change our lives? Imagine life over the centuries as it has been changed by various inventions.

1. We have can openers, with which we are able to open cans. Without can openers, *we wouldn't be able to open cans*.

2. By using forks and chopsticks, we don't have to use our fingers to eat. Without forks and chopsticks, _____.

3. Because electricity was discovered, we have electric lights, movies, television, and computers. Had electricity _____.

4. Jet planes did not exist in the last century; people did not travel extensively then. Had jet planes _____.

5. Television is available throughout the world; as a result, fashions, music, and basic values are very similar in many places. Were television _____.

6. Because computers were developed, businesses are able to obtain the data they need to function in today's competitive world. Had computers _____.

7. With computers, the general public has easy access to extensive knowledge. Without computers, _____.

5. Editing

Read the following passage. Find and correct the twelve errors in the forms of conditionals and subjunctives. Several of the conditional and subjunctive sentences are correct.

I have often fantasized about the perfect world. It would be perfect not only for my family and me, but for everyone.

First of all, ~~we were~~ *were we* living in a perfect world, there would be food for everyone. No one would be starving or without regular sources of food. Second, in this perfect world, everything would be clean and free of pollution. With clean air and toxin-free water, humans, animals, and plants would stayed healthy. Third, all diseases would be conquered; we will be free of cancer, AIDS, and heart disease. Without those diseases, people could lived longer and be free from terrible suffering. If had scientists already discovered a cure for these diseases, we could now be anticipating a much longer life span. Fourth, were the world in perfect condition, there will be no crime. Societal and psychological factors would not breed the crime that they do. And last, there would be no wars. All countries and all peoples would live together, harmoniously as one.

While these goals may appear unrealistic, it would be wise not to abandon them. Had statesmen abandoned the idea of one world, we don't have the United Nations today. Had scientists given up their search for cures, we will not have found the means to conquer polio, tuberculosis, some types of pneumonia, and many bacteria-caused diseases. Had civic-minded individuals been less tenacious, we did not have cleaned up the cities and waters and air as much as we have. Had we not learned and taught better methods of agriculture and food distribution, many more people would be starving today.

What if it were required by law that all of the *haves*—those people who *have* a decent life and more than enough material things—made concrete contributions to a perfect world? Local governments would require that citizens gave a specified amount of time or money each year to a recognized community project. Would such a program work? It could and should; otherwise, we would have to give up on making appreciable progress toward a better, if not perfect, world. It is absolutely essential that hope is expressed not only in theory, but also tangibly in order to improve the quality of all life on earth.

6. Personalization

What was the most serious problem you faced and how did you deal with it? How would you deal with a similar problem today? Write a short essay. Include some of the phrases in the box.

> One of the most serious problems I faced was . . .
>
> Had I known at the time that . . .
>
> It was essential that I . . .
>
> Without a lot of luck at that time, I . . .
>
> It's indeed fortunate that this happened. What if . . .
>
> Were a similar problem to arise now, I would . . .
>
> Were a similiar problem to arise, I might try to solve it in the same way. If so, . . . Otherwise, . . .
>
> Everyone faces problems like mine. Life demands that we . . .

Answer Key

Note: In this answer key, where the contracted form is given, the full form is also correct, and where the full form is given, the contracted form is also correct.

PART V: Adverbials and Discourse Connectors

 Adverb Clauses

1.

although family members may argue (contrast)   because every person needs to know that somebody cares for and about him or her (reason)   if a person feels connected to another (condition)   When family members have goals and support each other's goals (time)   if a parent is hoping to be promoted at work (condition)   If a youngster is trying to make the basketball team (condition)   When one family member is having trouble (time)   Even though this person doesn't have a job (contrast)   because this person doesn't have a job (reason)   so [secure] that they know their families will always be there for them (result)   wherever you look (place)

2.

2. as soon as 3. Wherever he goes 4. less expensive than 5. When you want 6. less than 7. If she likes 8. so fascinating that

3.

2. As soon as 3. Until 4. Wherever 5. even though 6. if 7. than 8. while 9. so

4.

2. Whenever we turn on the television, we are bombarded with scenes and stories of violence. OR We are bombarded with scenes and stories of violence whenever we turn on the television. 3. When we go out, we know it is possible that we will become victims of violence. OR We know it is possible that we will become victims of violence when we go out. 4. In spite of the fact that an ever-increasing amount of money is being spent on crime, crime rates have not fallen. OR Crime rates have not fallen in spite of the fact that an ever-increasing amount of money is being spent on crime. 5. As long as the public can't agree on how to fight crime, there is little that can really be done. OR There is little that can really be done as long as the public can't agree on how to fight crime. 6. Because we need to understand violence better, we are searching for its causes. 7. Since children in strong families tend to become socially responsible citizens, we need to take steps to strengthen the family. OR We need to take steps to strengthen the family since children in strong families tend to become socially responsible citizens.

5.

While animals on the lower end of the scale they display → While animals on the lower end of the scale display   If when we watch → If we watch/When we watch   because wherever conformity → because conformity   Whether the sport it is → Whether the sport is   long before became → long before it became   wherever was there enough space → wherever there was enough space   sports are of so interest that → sports are of such interest that   Although young people are especially interested → Because/Since/On account of the fact that young people are especially interested   Because that you want → Because you want

6.

(Answers will vary.)

UNIT 13 Adverbials: Viewpoint, Focus, and Negative

1.

Just almost Unfortunately hardly only almost scarcely Not only Never never Obviously Maybe simply Maybe merely Luckily rarely Actually really even clearly just Frankly at all Little even just Only

2.

2. But really he used up the state's money. OR But he really used up the state's money. **3.** He put only his cronies in the best jobs. **4.** He even paid for their so-called business trips. **5.** He did merely the minimal work. **6.** He simply appeared in his office, dispensed favors, and went out to play golf. **7.** He just didn't care about the people of this state. **8.** This state will be saved only if you elect Don Deare.

3.

2. Seldom does he take a vacation. **3.** Rarely is he able to spend much time with them. **4.** Never does he neglect his family. **5.** On no account would he accept a bribe. **6.** Only then does he make a decision. **7.** Little do people realize how many hours he has volunteered at the shelter for the homeless. **8.** Never does he think of himself first. **9.** Not only has he served the people very well as a civic volunteer, but he will do even more for them as a senator.

4.

2. We clearly agree that steps must be taken to strengthen the family. **3A.** Sadly, there is another factor that must be considered, however—the influence of TV violence. **B.** There is, sadly, another factor that must be considered, however—the influence of TV violence. **4.** We encounter scenes of violence wherever we look, even in cartoon shows and programs for families. **5A.** Unfortunately, our children can't help seeing these scenes. **B.** Our children, unfortunately, can't help seeing these scenes. **C.** Our children can't help seeing these scenes, unfortunately. **6.** Not only must we take action to strengthen the family, but we must pressure our legislators to stop TV violence. **7A.** Obviously, much needs to be done. **B.** Much needs to be done, obviously. **C.** Much, obviously, needs to be done. **8A.** Hopefully, we will win the war against violent programs. **B.** We will, hopefully, win the war against violent programs. **C.** We will win the war against violent programs, hopefully. **9A.** Fortunately, we can limit our children's TV viewing. **B.** We can, fortunately, limit our children's TV viewing. **C.** We can limit our children's TV viewing, fortunately. **10.** This means allowing only programs that do not show violence. **11.** Other programs are, simply, "off limits." **12.** We also have to help our children develop interests so they will not be tempted at all to sit glued to the TV. OR We also have to help our children develop interests so they will not be at all tempted to sit glued to the TV. OR We also have to help our children develop interests so they will not at all be tempted to sit glued to the TV.

5.

battling hard really → really battling hard/battling really hard   the only best players → only the best players   seldom amateurs appear → seldom do amateurs appear/amateurs seldom appear   is to simply score → is simply to score   A player hopefully gets → Hopefully, a player gets   is as just fierce as → is just as fierce as   never gives nothing → never gives anything   is won through only a hard fight → is won only through a hard fight   not only it is necessary → not only is it necessary   To obviously know the words is important → Obviously, to know the words is important/To know the words is important, obviously/To know the words, obviously, is important   is more even important → is even more important   know how just to place the letters → know just how to place the letters   even there is → there is even   At all this is not the image → This is not at all the image   mathematical wizards play only this game → only mathematical wizards play this game   One hundred sixty-seven actually different occupations → Actually, 167 different occupations   Little it is known → Little is it known   as just vigorously as → just as vigorously as

6.

(Answers will vary.)

UNIT 14 Other Discourse Connectors

1.

As a result   Moreover   In addition   therefore   However   In fact   Next   but   so   besides that   nevertheless   Finally   For one thing   and   along with   On the other hand   or   and   Meanwhile

2.

2. but **3.** As a result **4.** First **5.** Second **6.** Third **7.** for example **8.** To sum up **9.** in contrast **10.** and **11.** Also

3.

2. but **3.** in fact **4.** As a result **5.** Furthermore **6.** In contrast **7.** Moreover **8.** so **9.** nor

4.

2. Instead **3.** First **4.** Otherwise **5.** In addition **6.** And **7.** finally **8.** so **9.** Despite **10.** For instance **11.** Along with **12.** but **13.** Besides

5.

The following answers are suggested. In some cases other answers are possible. however → but   Because → Therefore/Consequently   and → also/in addition   or → nor   however the fact → despite the fact   also → and

nevertheless → but   but → however   Although → However   consequently → because of

6.

(Answers will vary.)

UNIT 15 Adverbial Modifying Phrases

1.

While struggling with the demands presented by a population grown too fast
creating more problems than solutions
Having caused such strains that our government can no longer effectively serve us
by limiting the number of high-density buildings permitted to be built in certain areas
by discouraging outsiders from investing in our city
By taking concrete measures like these
Faced with a tough choice between limiting our population and letting our standards of living slip

2.

2. Having been **3.** Having lost **4.** To ensure **5.** not having **6.** stressed **7.** spreading **8.** bringing

3.

2. Having been told . . . /Told that vitamin C, vitamin E, and beta-carotene greatly reduce cancer risk, people began buying these nutrients in large quantities. **3.** Informed that taking one aspirin a day lessens the chances of having a heart attack, people began taking aspirin. **4.** Having learned that one glass of wine per day has a beneficial effect on the heart and circulatory system, many people now drink wine for medicinal reasons. **5.** Hoping to lower their cholesterol levels, people minimize their intake of animal fats. **6.** Knowing that roughage in the diet is excellent for digestion, people are consuming more fresh fruit, vegetables, and whole wheat products. **7.** Believing that eating a lot of fish will raise their intelligence level, some people eat a lot of fish. **8.** Having known for a long time that too much salt and sugar is unhealthful, people buy a lot of salt-free and sugar-free products. **9.** Realizing that they can contribute to their own good health, people eat much more knowledgeably than they used to.

4.

Found → Finding   to continued → to continue   After having complete → After having completed   When look → When looking   Having find → Having found   to clicking → by clicking   Having join → Having joined   When require → When required   Have obtained → Having obtained   while have → while having

5.

(Answers will vary.)

PART VI: Adjective Clauses

UNIT 16 Review and Expansion

1.

you make when writing or typing
who began using tempera paint to cover up her typing errors
whose ink didn't erase as cleanly as that of manual typewriters
who was also an artist
which she called Mistake Out
she had bought for the backyard
which turned her down
which came to be called Liquid Paper
which ended about six months before she sold the company
of which $3.5 million was net income
she finally sold her business to Gilette in 1979
of whom she is understandably proud
which appeared on an NBC television show for several years in the mid-1960s
where he also directs some charities
whose purpose is to provide leading intellectuals with the time, space, and compatible colleagues
that they need to ponder and articulate the most important social problems of our era
that there was clearly a need for
which is a fine thing to do

2.

2. which **3.** where **4.** who/that **5.** which/that **6.** whom/that/0 **7.** which/that/0 **8.** that/which/0 **9.** whose **10.** who/that **11.** when **12.** which **13.** which/that **14.** which/that **15.** which/that **16.** which/that/0

3.

2. H A beeper is a battery-operated device whose beeping noise indicates when someone is trying to make a phone connection with you. **3.** E An air bag is a device in a car that/which inflates upon collision to prevent injury. **4.** J A microwave oven is an oven in which people cook food quickly./A microwave oven is an oven that/which/0 people cook food quickly in. **5.** A A fax machine is a machine that/which transmits written material instantly by telephone. **6.** G A computer is an electronic device whose function is to store and process data. **7.** I A CD is a small disc on which music is recorded./A CD is a small disc that/which/0 music is recorded on. **8.** B An answering machine is an electronic device that/which records telephone messages. **9.** D An electronic dictionary is a gadget in which you find words by punching in their letters./An electronic dictionary is a gadget that/which/0 you find words in by punching in their letters. **10.** C A VCR is a machine that/which records TV shows for viewing at a future time.

4.

2. B **3.** A **4.** B **5.** A **6.** B **7.** A **8.** B **9.** A **10.** A **11.** B **12.** B

5.

some of them → some of which   whom is nervous → who is nervous   whom rarely smiles → who rarely smiles   to which everything is serious → to whom everything is serious   who they are → who are   whom often suffered → who often suffered   of that others → of whom others   which is probably not → who is probably not   they were born under it → they were born under   who born → who was born   that born → that was born   that are intuitive → who are intuitive   who they are → who are   whose his brain → whose brain   to improve it → to improve   for people are looking → for people who are looking   which it is → which is

6.

(Answers will vary.)

UNIT 17 Adjective Clauses with Quantifiers; Adjectival Modifying Phrases

1.

Adjective Clauses: many of which were filmed in remote parts of the world   one of which was called *A Trip to the Moon* and influenced many subsequent filmmakers   some of which involved chase scenes

Adjective Phrases: learning how to fake prizefights, news events, and foreign settings   made with the aid of the microscope   credited with creating methods   leading toward the development of special-effects movies   shot outdoors   a camera operator and director   showing different actions simultaneously   seen and loved even today   changing the world forever

2.

2. most of which could have been avoided **3.** half of which are longer than 40 days **4.** 71 percent of whom think people in power take advantage of others **5.** 14 percent of whom achieve scores of over 130 on IQ tests **6.** more than half of whom are under 64 years old **7.** all of which yield more nutrients when lightly cooked than when raw **8.** much of which is junk food

3.

2. embodied by Catherine Deneuve as a plantation owner **3.** surrounding her **4.** transformed by a magic spell **5.** reunited for a funeral **6.** raising a lion cub in Kenya **7.** enlisted to impersonate the president of the United States **8.** falling into trouble as they emigrate to America **9.** held in captivity **10.** fighting to save Africa's gorillas from extinction **11.** again separated from his vacationing family   facing similar woes **12.** becoming involved with a wealthy family

4.

2. Then, there are various places where you can buy computers, including computer stores, electronics stores, office supply stores, and mail-order houses. **3.** At reasonable prices, ranging from $1,200 to $3,000, you can get everything you need. **4.** Within this price range, of course, you will find varying capabilities among the computers, many of which come equipped with a fax/modem. **5.** Many major brands of computer have a toll-free number, given to customers so that they may call the company for technical assistance. **6.** If you are a new buyer, having little experience with computers, you should buy from a store where you know you can get help. **7.** While you are shopping around, you will find words like *hard drive, megabyte,* and *CD-ROM drive,* all of which are part of a computer owner's vocabulary. **8.** If you need your computer while you're traveling, you should consider a laptop, small enough and light enough to carry with you. **9.** Sometimes computers come with programs already installed at the factory. **10.** You don't have to buy many extra capabilities, unneeded by beginners, right away. **11.** For newcomers to computers, it's a good idea to take some classes or to get a tutor, both of which can usually be arranged for by the store.

PART VII: Noun Clauses

UNIT 18 — Noun Clauses: Subjects and Objects

1.

that ruthlessness in modern war is necessary
that sacrificing one's life and the lives of others is glorious
That all a nation's able-bodied men give compulsory military service
whoever was able
What took place in the United States
why people go to war
whether any territorial imperative, commercial advantage, or religious belief can justify the loss of even one life
whatever we can to end conscription everywhere
that no cause, however just, is rationale enough to force a man to fight to kill

2.

2. Who talked to the boss about Charlie 3. Where Charlie is now 4. When Charlie is going to be arrested 5. When the money was stolen 6. What will happen to Charlie 7. Whether or not Charlie is a thief 8. we have a big-time embezzler in our company 9. What I think about this news

5.

making in 1945 → made in 1945   that produced for entertainment value → produced for entertainment value   showed the harshness of life → showing the harshness of life   was an outstanding director → an outstanding director   the most famous of them is → the most famous of which is   which a movie → a movie   calling the "New Wave" → called the "New Wave"   seeing in movies → seen in movies   was known as the "Angry Young Man" movement → known as the "Angry Young Man" movement

some of them are masterfully explored → some of which are masterfully explored   was the first Asian filmmaker → the first Asian filmmaker   portray the problems of the individual → portraying the problems of the individual   included Shakespeare's plays → including Shakespeare's plays   many of them were focusing → many of which were focusing

6.

(Answers will vary.)

3.

2. that a school's curriculum should include a strong sports program 3. what students can do to become part of a team 4. whoever is interested in a sport and tries hard 5. whatever training is necessary 6. that the training is difficult 7. what he or she has to do 8. where he or she belongs 9. what it feels like to be a team player

4.

how does a person find → how a person finds   concluded that is it → concluded that it is   questioned what were the real values in life → questioned what the real values in life were   whomever opposed → whoever opposed   feel that war it → feel that war   whatever convictions do they personally hold → whatever convictions they personally hold   for that would normally be → for what would normally be   for whatever in the world → for wherever in the world

5.

(Answers will vary.)

UNIT 19 — Complementation

1.

(that) a direct way of speaking is more effective than an indirect way of speaking and is also a sign of power and self-confidence (adjective complement)
that the degree of directness of speech varies greatly among cultures (subject complement)
that both women and men are indirect (adjective complement)
that directness always works best (adjective complement)
that one of the subordinates will close the window right away (subject complement)

that the subordinate quickly find and present the information (adjective complement)
that more than the choice of vocabulary and tone of voice determine whether a command is successful (adjective complement)
that the status of the speaker and the listener be mutually understood (subject complement)
that both people interact in accordance with the unwritten rules of this understanding (subject complement)

2.

2. that I forget about Lisa 3. that this is much easier said than done 4. that I can't forget about her 5. that I am not receptive to meeting people 6. that I get my life in order 7. that you be responsible on the job 8. that you have always been too casual about your work 9. that you keep the next job you get 10. that you adopt a better attitude 11. that you not invest any more money in bad deals

3.

2. C It is necessary that time be taken to do a job right. 3. F It is advisable that you not criticize others for faults you have. 4. H It is essential that things be done in the right order. 5. B It is advisable that problems be taken care of before they get worse. 6. I It is important that you not be upset over what already happened. 7. G It is desirable that a person stick with what he or she already has rather than going after other things. 8. A It is vital that a person enjoy life as well as work. 9. D It is essential that a person get an early start to beat the competition. 10. J It is necessary that precautions be taken *before* there is trouble.

4.

The fact it is that students → The fact is that students   If it is clear that experiencing Mozart raise → If it is clear that experiencing Mozart raises   in the background it seems clear → in the background seems clear   obvious to the parents because that → obvious to the parents that   insist that the child listens → insist that the child listen   insist that something is done → insist that something be done   problem is it that → problem is that

5.

(Answers will vary.)

PART VIII: Unreal Conditions

UNIT 20: Unreal Conditionals and Other Ways to Express Unreality

1.

If he hadn't, the delicious substance might never have crossed the ocean to Spain.

If it hadn't been so expensive, the masses could have enjoyed it much sooner.

If this chocolatier hadn't, we would not have the wide range of candies and candy bars that we have today.

If he hadn't, Switzerland and the Netherlands would not have become the great producers of quality chocolates that they are.

if he hadn't, we would not have chocolate cakes or chocolate chip cookies.

if there were not such a well-developed world trade, chocolate lovers would not be ale to indulge themselves so easily.

if their fat and sugar intake were lower, they would be healthier.

". . . if I had a day without chocolate, it would be like a day without sunshine."

2.

2. was brought back to Europe by the Spanish explorers   is popular today 3. are not healthy   eat a lot of chocolate and other foods containing fat and sugar 4. don't eat a balanced diet   are not well nourished 5. have enough willpower to refuse junk food 6. consumed 4,000 calories at the last meal that they ate 7. is a tomorrow 8. isn't easy

3.

2. I met the right man, I would have a different feeling about it 3. I didn't have a lot of friends, I would be lonely 4. I didn't like my job, I would be unhappy 5. (that) people would leave me alone 6. I were a weird person 7. I could meet the perfect man tomorrow 8. (that) I had it all/I could have it all 9. (that) I meet somebody 10. that's an excellent matchmaking service 11. they introduce me to someone perfect

4.

2. would never have met 3. would have failed 4. hadn't wasted 5. wouldn't have had to eat 6. would have known 7. wouldn't have been 8. wouldn't have suffered 9. had met 10. hadn't fallen asleep 11. wouldn't have been able to 12. had never met 13. hadn't happened 14. hadn't made 15. would have passed

5.

would called her up → would call her up   would never had met → would never have met   wish we have already been → wish we had already been   as though I knew her → as though I'd known her/as though I've known her   would liked her → would like her   what did she say → what would she say   as though we are kids → as though we were kids   hope that you answered → hope that you answer

6.

(Answers will vary.)

Unit 21: Inverted and Implied Conditionals; Subjunctive in Noun Clauses

1.

Without (the simple little tool that we take for granted)
(essential that we) have
What if (we had no way of preserving . . .)
Without (canned tuna)
if not (used correctly)
Had the U.S. military not adopted this primitive can opener in the Civil War . . .
otherwise (we would not have the convenience . . .)

2.

2. that he or she drive on the left 3. that people remove their shoes before going inside a house 4. that people keep their shoes on 5. that people not eat pork products 6. that pork products be avoided 7. that a sick person take vitamin C 8. that a sick person have a lot of homemade chicken soup 9. that a waiter be summoned by whistling 10. that a waiter not be summoned by whistling 11. that a traveler learn about customs in various places

3.

2. not gained, would have remained 3. might not have won 4. would not have grown 5. rejected, would not have become 6. not won, would have gained 7. would have died 8. lived, would have served

4.

2. we would have to use our fingers to eat 3. not been discovered, we wouldn't have electric lights, movies, television, or computers 4. existed in the last century, people would have traveled extensively then 5. not available throughout the world, fashion, music, and basic values would not be very similar in many places 6. not been developed, businesses wouldn't be able to obtain the data they need to function in today's competitive world. 7. the general public wouldn't have easy access to extensive knowledge

5.

plants would stayed healthy → plants would stay healthy   we will be free → we would be free   people could lived longer → people could live longer   If had scientists already discovered → Had scientists already discovered/If scientists had already discovered   there will be no crime → there would be no crime   we don't have the United Nations → we wouldn't have the United Nations   we will not have found the means → we would not have found the means   we did not have cleaned up → we would not have cleaned up   that the *haves* . . . made concrete contributions → that the *haves* . . . make concrete contributions   that citizens gave a specified amount → that citizens give a specified amount   that hope is expressed → that hope be expressed

6.

(Answers will vary.)

TEST: UNITS 12–15

PART ONE

DIRECTIONS: Circle the letter of the correct answer to complete each sentence.

Example:

Dolphins, _____ porpoises, are well known for their ability to delight humans with their antics.

   A   B   (C)   D

- A. alike
- B. that they are like
- C. like
- D. which are alike

1. Never before in the history of the country _____ as spiritually united as they were during the war.

   A   B   C   D

- A. the people were
- B. the people had been
- C. had the people been
- D. when the people were

2. The Industrial Revolution created a great need for labor in factories in cities; _____ the population became increasingly less rural and more urban.

   A   B   C   D

- A. so that
- B. consequently,
- C. nevertheless,
- D. otherwise,

TEST: UNITS 12–15

3. The Twenty-second Amendment to the Constitution of the United States provides for a limitation of the president's time of service, stating that _____ two terms in office.

A. only the president is limited to

B. the president is limited to only

C. the president is only limited to

D. the president only is limited to

4. Although most citizens desire extensive services from their government, _____ is willing to pay higher taxes.

A. but nobody

B. nobody

C. however, nobody

D. so nobody

5. During solar eclipses, people are advised to view the sun directly only while _____ through a very small hole in a piece of cardboard.

A. they have been looking

B. looked

C. looking

D. having looked

6. In the last senatorial election, _____ voted for the current senator.

A. 60 percent of the population almost

B. almost 60 percent of the population

C. 60 percent of the population hardly

D. not only 60 percent of the population

7. _____ expenses are so much higher in certain cities than in others, companies must provide higher salaries to its employees in those places.

A. Since

B. Although

C. Because of

D. Only

8. It is projected that by the year 2010, there will be _____ people over the age of 65 that the monies from Social Security won't be sufficient to support them.

A. such

B. so

C. too many

D. so many

9. Wherever overbuilding has taken place along the coast of the barrier islands, _____ erosion is occurring.

A. so beach

B. consequently beach

C. beach

D. so that beach

10. Learning to play a musical instrument often motivates a child to be disciplined and effective; _____ it can impart a feeling of social worth.

A. but

B. because

C. so

D. moreover,

T 4 ▼ TEST: UNITS 12–15

PART TWO

DIRECTIONS: *Each sentence has four underlined words or phrases. The four underlined parts of the sentence are marked A, B, C, and D. Circle the letter of the one underlined word or phrase that is NOT CORRECT.*

Example:

People in <u>every part</u> of the world now <u>readily</u> and easily   A   B   Ⓒ   D
            A   B
<u>communicates</u> <u>by means</u> of electronic mail.
       C   D

11. <u>Little</u> <u>Columbus did</u> know, <u>crossing</u> the Atlantic in 1492, that his   A   B   C   D
     A   B   C
    voyage <u>would</u> change the course of history forever.
            D

12. Halley's Comet appears <u>so rarely</u> that <u>only do a few</u> people <u>have</u>   A   B   C   D
                          A   B   C
    the opportunity to view it more <u>than once</u> in a lifetime.
                                 D

13. <u>Few children</u>, <u>fortunately</u>, get diseases like polio, scarlet fever,   A   B   C   D
     A   B
    and whooping cough <u>anymore</u>, <u>because of</u> immunization
                         C   D
    programs are widespread.

14. <u>Cellular telephones</u> are now <u>such convenient</u> that a business   A   B   C   D
         A   B
    person can and <u>often does save</u> valuable office time by efficiently
                       C
    making telephone calls <u>while driving</u>.
                          D

15. <u>Not only</u> <u>the supply of mahogany has</u> dwindled markedly in the   A   B   C   D
      A   B
    past ten years, but <u>its price has</u> tripled during the same period
                    C
    <u>of time</u>.
     D

16. <u>Having begun</u> his career <u>as a journalist</u>, Federico Fellini   A   B   C   D
      A   B
    became a renowned film director and <u>writer, and</u> winning several
                                 C
    prestigious awards for his <u>works</u>.
                          D

17. <u>When was first setting foot</u> on the moon, Neil Armstrong spoke to   A   B   C   D
           A
    the entire world <u>by</u> television satellite and said that <u>the event</u> was
                B   C
    a giant leap for <u>mankind</u>.
                   D

18. <u>Having retiring</u> from playing professional tennis, Chris Evert is
       A

now seen <u>commenting</u> on tennis matches <u>and</u> <u>also</u> advertising
         B   C   D

certain products.

A   B   C   D

19. <u>Because</u> Finland is part of Scandinavia, <u>its</u> language is, <u>in fact</u>,
       A   B   C

not like those of the other Scandinavian countries <u>at all</u>.
                                                   D

A   B   C   D

20. <u>Reflected</u> economic conditions as well as social attitudes, the
       A

immigration laws continue <u>to change</u> in order <u>to admit</u> certain
                          B   C

people and <u>refuse entry</u> to others.
           D

A   B   C   D

TEST: UNITS 16–17

PART ONE

DIRECTIONS: Circle the letter of the correct answer to complete each sentence.

Example:

Dolphins, _____ porpoises, are well known for their ability to delight humans with their antics.   A   B   Ⓒ   D

   A. alike

   B. that they are like

   C. like

   D. which are alike

1. Tulips, _____ into Holland in 1554, were quickly and highly valued and soon became the object of wild financial speculation in Europe.   A   B   C   D

   A. which introduced

   B. that they were introduced

   C. which introduced them

   D. introduced

2. Concepts of modern nursing were founded by Florence Nightingale, an English nurse _____ to the care of the sick and the war-wounded.   A   B   C   D

   A. that she dedicated her life

   B. whose life she dedicated

   C. whose life was dedicated

   D. whose life she dedicated it

3. Relics _____ accidentally while constructing a new subway line in Mexico City yielded new information about previous civilizations in the area.

A. that workers found them

B. which workers they found

C. that they were found by workers

D. that workers found

A   B   C   D

4. The advanced course in astrophysics will be open only to those graduate students _____ a grade point average of 3.8 or above.

A. have

B. they will have

C. having

D. whom have

A   B   C   D

5. Cork, the second largest city in Ireland, is the site of many industries, _____ automobile manufacturing and whiskey distilling.

A. some of them are

B. which some are

C. some of which are

D. of which are some

A   B   C   D

6. Ships traveling in the North Atlantic during the winter must be constantly vigilant to avoid icebergs, large masses of ice _____ only one-ninth is visible above water.

A. that

B. of that

C. which

D. of which

A   B   C   D

7. The Olympic Games, _____ in 776 B.C., did not include women participants until 1912.   A   B   C   D

A. they were first played

B. that they were first played

C. which first played

D. first played

8. One of the great fiction writers in English, Charles Dickens wrote about all kinds of societal abuses, _____ child labor, debt imprisonment, and legal injustices.   A   B   C   D

A. which are including

B. that they include

C. included

D. including

9. *The Mikado,* a warm-hearted spoof of a country _____, is one of the best loved works of the English operetta composers Gilbert and Sullivan.   A   B   C   D

A. which they knew nothing about

B. that they knew nothing about it

C. about that they knew nothing

D. they know nothing about it

10. Few visitors to Disney World are aware that much of its electrical power comes from the energy _____ by burning its own garbage.   A   B   C   D

A. that produces

B. producing

C. which it is produced

D. it produces

PART TWO

DIRECTIONS: Each sentence has four underlined words or phrases. The four underlined parts of the sentence are marked A, B, C, and D. Circle the letter of the one underlined word or phrase that is NOT CORRECT.

Example:

People in every part of the world now readily and easily   A   B   Ⓒ   D
               A   B

communicates by means of electronic mail.
       C   D

11. A famous Danish writer who wrote mainly in English, Isak   A   B   C   D
                                A

    Dinesen is best known for her imaginative tales which containing
                  B   C   D

    romantic and supernatural elements.

12. Sunlight sometimes filters through rain droplets in a way that forms   A   B   C   D
                                          A

    a rainbow, which it is an arc composed of every color in the
               B   C

    spectrum and often is regarded as an omen of good luck.
                      D

13. Japanese, which spoken by more than 100 million people,   A   B   C   D
                A

    most of whom live in Japan, appears to be unrelated to any other
          B   C

    language spoken in Asia.
                D

14. Genius is a term which may be used to describe a person whom has   A   B   C   D
                   A   B

    a high intelligence or possesses a special aptitude for
                       C

    excelling in a particular field.
     D

15. In a medical study of nearly 5,000 adults, half of who were given   A   B   C   D
                                        A

    one aspirin a day while the other half were given a placebo, it was
                                       B

    found that those who were taking the aspirin suffered 38 percent
              C

    fewer heart attacks than those who weren't.
                              D

16. A fact not widely known is that Theodore Roosevelt, that was a   A   B   C   D
      A   B   C

    robust and boisterous outdoorsman, had been a weak and sickly

    child who suffered from asthma.
          D

17. Educated women in the last decades of the twentieth century have
been marrying later, which that means that they have fewer
            A   B   C
years in which to produce offspring.
         D

18. Among the stalwart Indians who defeated General George Custer
                                 A
in 1876 was Crazy Horse, a Sioux who, resisted encroachment of
                                 B   C
his lands, had repeatedly defeated U.S. troops in previous battles.
                  D

19. Lagos, the capital and largest city of Nigeria, which is comprised
                                                       A
of four islands and four inland sections, all of which are connected
B   C   D
by bridges.

20. Many older couples, whose children have grown and left home,
                         A
move to retirement villages, in where they can participate in
                              B
activities they enjoy and meet people with whom they have
   C   D
much in common.

TEST: UNITS 18–19

PART ONE

DIRECTIONS: Circle the letter of the correct answer to complete each sentence.

Example:

Dolphins, _____ porpoises, are well known for their ability to delight humans with their antics.   A   B   Ⓒ   D

  A. alike
  B. that they are like
  C. like
  D. which are alike

1. In order to avert disaster, it is essential _____ of the dangers of avalanches in the area.   A   B   C   D

  A. that travelers be advised
  B. that travelers they are advised
  C. advising travelers
  D. where to advise travelers

2. _____ the young woman chose to marry didn't matter, for she had to marry someone that her parents had selected.   A   B   C   D

  A. Whomever
  B. Whatever
  C. Whoever was
  D. Whoever was that

TEST: UNITS 18–19 ▼ T 11

3. _____ the ozone layer has already thinned to a dangerous point is a serious problem.

A. What

B. That

C. It is a fact that

D. Scientists know that

4. It is clear _____ the city government will have to raise taxes if the police force is going to be strengthened.

A. what

B. that

C. whatever

D. whether

5. It is generally considered unwise to give a child _____ he or she wants.

A. whatever is it

B. that

C. whatever that

D. whatever

6. Organic food companies stress _____ no pesticides or other harmful products are used in growing their products.

A. what

B. neither

C. both

D. that

7. After the flood had left so many homeless, the neighboring towns-people donated _____ of their food, clothing and shelter.

A. however could they spare

B. whichever they can spare

C. whatever they could spare

D. what they spared

8. Both gubernatorial candidates are well qualified, so that _____ will serve the state well.

A. whom is elected

B. whomever is elected

C. whoever is elected

D. whichever elects

9. _____ the mathematical ability of girls is innately the same as that of boys has still not been universally accepted.

A. It is a fact that

B. In fact,

C. The fact that

D. The fact is that

10. Dermatologists are recommending that people with fair skin _____ a strong sun screen.

A. use

B. that they use

C. to use

D. are using

T 14 ▼ TEST: UNITS 18–19

PART TWO

DIRECTIONS: Each sentence has four underlined words or phrases. The four underlined parts of the sentence are marked A, B, C, and D. Circle the letter of the one underlined word or phrase that is NOT CORRECT.

Example:

People in <u>every part</u> of the world now <u>readily</u> and easily   A   B   Ⓒ   D
          A   B
<u>communicates</u> <u>by means</u> of electronic mail.
    C   D

11. <u>That</u> spurred the great explorations of the fifteenth and sixteenth   A   B   C   D
    A
centuries was the <u>desire to find</u> <u>a more</u> expeditious route to
                          B   C
<u>the spice</u> supplies of the Far East.
    D

12. Market researchers find out exactly <u>how many</u> <u>people live</u> in a   A   B   C   D
                                       A   B
certain area and <u>what</u> <u>are their spending habits</u>.
                C   D

13. The belief <u>what</u> a person <u>gets</u> what he or she <u>deserves</u> in this   A   B   C   D
             A   B   C
world <u>persists</u> despite evidence to the contrary.
      D

14. Urban sprawl occurred <u>wherever</u> <u>the population expanded</u>   A   B   C   D
                           A   B
rapidly and <u>where</u> <u>were there</u> no comprehensive plans for
            C   D
dealing with the situation.

15. <u>What is clear</u> is the <u>fact that</u> the mediocre level of popular   A   B   C   D
     A   B
television programming is based on <u>what do</u> advertisers think
                                 C
<u>the viewers want</u> to see.
    D

16. In spite of <u>the fact that</u> doctors have recommended strongly <u>that</u>   A   B   C   D
            A   B
adults <u>refrained</u> <u>from smoking</u> near children, such warnings have
        C   D
largely gone unheeded.

17. <u>Whatever</u> the individuals felt before attending the group therapy   A   B   C   D
    A
sessions, <u>it was clear</u> <u>that</u> <u>did they leave</u> the course with renewed
         B   C   D
hope.

18. The coach insists that the players <u>do</u> <u>whatever</u> <u>it is</u> necessary
                                        A   B   C

    <u>to win</u> the game.
      D

              A   **B**   **C**   **D**

19. The demonstrators for prison reform <u>demanded</u> that all the
                                                       A

    inequities of the system <u>were</u> <u>addressed</u> <u>before the day ended</u>.
                                  B   C   D

              A   **B**   **C**   **D**

20. The problem with the new, more equitable income taxes <u>is</u>
                                                                     A

    <u>because</u> they don't satisfy <u>demands that</u> all possible loopholes
      B   C

    <u>be eliminated</u>.
      D

              A   **B**   **C**   **D**

TEST: UNITS 20-21

PART ONE

DIRECTIONS: Circle the letter of the correct answer to complete each sentence.

Example:

Dolphins, _____ porpoises, are well known for   A   B   Ⓒ   D
their ability to delight humans with their antics.

  A. alike

  B. that they are like

  C. like

  D. which are alike

1. Without the help of the Indians of the area, the Pilgrims in   A   B   C   D

    Massachusetts _____ able to celebrate their

    first Thanksgiving.

  A. would never had been

  B. would never have been

  C. had never been

  D. they were never

2. Had the Spanish remained in North America, Canadians and   A   B   C   D

    Americans _____ Spanish now instead of English.

  A. would have spoken

  B. would be speaking

  C. have been speaking

  D. had been speaking

3. Corporate interests would not have voted for the Republican candidate if _____ considerable tax reductions.   A   B   C   D

A. she did not promise

B. she had not promised

C. she hasn't promised

D. she were not to promise

4. It is clear that John didn't make a good impression at his job interview; if so, the firm _____ him by now.   A   B   C   D

A. would call

B. would called

C. call

D. would have called

5. Although having difficulty in obtaining a license to operate a cable television channel, the station owners still hope that they _____ one this year.   A   B   C   D

A. will procure

B. would procure

C. were to procure

D. have procured

6. The crash victims probably would have died _____ arrived at the scene of the accident within minutes of its occurrence.   A   B   C   D

A. if had the ambulance not

B. did the ambulance not

C. if the ambulance would not have

D. had the ambulance not

7. Travel films have long been popular among people who would like to travel around the world and wish _____ the money to do so.

A. they have

B. they will have

C. they had

D. had they had

8. In certain types of mental illness, when a person speaks _____ a king, he truly believes that he is a king even if he is, in reality, a working man.

A. if he is

B. as though he be

C. as he was

D. as though he were

9. It is essential that _____ enough rain before the month ends if the area is to produce adequate coffee crops.

A. there be

B. there have

C. there should be

D. it has

10. A peaceful demonstration is anticipated, but the riot squad will remain ready to act _____ .

A. if should occur unexpected violence

B. that unexpected violence occurs

C. should unexpected violence occur

D. were to occur unexpected violence

TEST: UNITS 20–21 ▼ T 19

PART TWO

DIRECTIONS: Each sentence has four underlined words or phrases. The four underlined parts of the sentence are marked A, B, C, and D. Circle the letter of the one underlined word or phrase that is NOT CORRECT.

Example:

People in <u>every part</u> of the world now <u>readily</u> and easily   A   B   Ⓒ   D
             A   B
<u>communicates</u> <u>by means</u> of electronic mail.
      C   D

11. <u>If environmental groups</u> <u>have not exerted</u> pressure, <u>it is</u> almost   A   B   C   D
                  A   B   C
     certain that pandas <u>would now be</u> extinct.
                              D

12. Many people <u>have expressed</u> the concern <u>that a</u> problem <u>should</u>   A   B   C   D
                      A   B   C
     <u>develop</u> at a nuclear facility, the results <u>would be</u> disastrous.
       D

13. <u>It was</u> fortunate for the actress <u>that she had</u> already worked   A   B   C   D
      A   B
     with the director; otherwise, she <u>will</u> never <u>have been</u> awarded
                                     C   D
     the leading role.

14. Many people <u>buying</u> lottery tickets every week <u>believe</u> that if   A   B   C   D
                     A   B
     only they <u>have</u> a lot of money, their lives <u>would be</u> perfect.
              C   D

15. If the president <u>were become</u> incapacitated, specific constitutional   A   B   C   D
                          A
     procedures to install the vice president <u>would have to be</u> implemented
                                                     B
     quickly <u>so that</u> the leadership of the country <u>would remain</u> intact.
                C   D

16. In the days of the American pioneer, <u>it was</u> vital that the wagons   A   B   C   D
                                              A
     <u>crossing</u> the great prairies <u>carry</u> guns; otherwise, the occupants
        B   C
     <u>had been</u> helpless against wild animals or attacks by Indians.
       D

17. <u>Many a spirited</u> young person <u>who plays</u> practical jokes in his   A   B   C   D
         A   B
     teens later <u>wishes that</u> he <u>has behaved</u> in a more mature manner.
                   C   D

18. Queen Elizabeth <u>would never have</u> become <u>the</u> queen of England
                              A   B

   <u>if had not her uncle</u>, Edward VIII, renounced the throne <u>to marry</u>
         C   D

   a commoner.

    A   B   C   D

19. <u>By suggesting</u> that a softer approach toward the <u>opposing</u> party
       A   B

   <u>were adopted</u>, the lawyer hoped <u>to effect</u> a decent settlement for
      C   D

   his client.

    A   B   C   D

20. <u>Had the South</u> <u>defeated</u> the North in the American Civil War in
        A   B

   1865, the industrial development of the country <u>would proceed</u>
                                                              C

   more slowly than <u>it did</u>.
                    D

    A   B   C   D

ANSWER KEY FOR TEST: UNITS 12–15

Note: Correct responses for Part Two questions appear in parentheses.

PART ONE

1. C   2. B   3. B   4. B   5. C   6. B   7. A   8. D   9. C   10. D

PART TWO

11. B (did Columbus)   12. B (only a few)   13. D (because)   14. B (so convenient)
15. B (has the supply of mahogany)   16. C (writer)   17. A (When [he was] first setting foot)
18. A (Having retired)   19. A (Although)   20. A (Reflecting)

ANSWER KEY FOR TEST: UNITS 16–17

PART ONE

1. D   2. C   3. D   4. C   5. C   6. D   7. D   8. D   9. A   10. D

PART TWO

11. D (containing/that contain/which contain)   12. B (which is)   13. A (is spoken)
14. B (who has)   15. A (half of whom)   16. C (who was)   17. B (means)
18. C (resisting)   19. A (0—omit *which*)   20. B (in which/where)

ANSWER KEY FOR TEST: UNITS 18–19

PART ONE

1. A   2. A   3. B   4. B   5. D   6. D   7. C   8. C   9. C   10. A

PART TWO

11. A (What)   12. D (their spending habits are)   13. A (that)   14. D (there were)
15. C (what)   16. C (refrain)   17. D (they left)   18. C (is)   19. B (be)   20. B (that)

ANSWER KEY FOR TEST: UNITS 20–21

PART ONE

1. B   2. B   3. B   4. D   5. A   6. D   7. C   8. D   9. A   10. C

PART TWO

11. B (had not exerted)   12. B (that if a)   13. C (would)   14. C (had)
15. A (were to become)   16. D (would have been)   17. D (had behaved)
18. C (had not her uncle)   19. C (be adopted)   20. C (would have proceded)